3 8002 01729 018 2

COVENTRY LIBRARIES

Please return this book on or before
the last date stamped below.

Central

02 JUL 2010

To renew this book take it to any of
the City Libraries before
the date due for return

Coventry City Council

D1437936

Also by Angelika Wolk-Gerche:

Papercraft

More Magic Wool

Angelika Wolk-Gerche

Creative Felt

Felting and Making More Toys and Gifts

Floris Books

Translated by Anna Cardwell
Photographs by Wolpert & Strehle, Dieter Wolk
Drawings by Angelika Wolk-Gerche

First published in German under the titles Filzen für Gross und Klein and Spielzeug filzen
by Verlag Freies Geistesleben.
First published in English as Creative Felt in 2007 by Floris Books
Revised edition published by Floris Books in 2009
(c) 1996 and 2003 Verlag Freies Geistesleben & Urachhaus GmbH, Stuttgart
English version (c) Floris Books 2009

All rights reserved. No part of this publication may be reproduced without the
prior permission of Floris Books, 15 Harrison Gardens, Edinburgh. www.florisbooks.co.uk

Coventry City Council	
CEN	
3 8002 01729 018 2	
Askews	Nov-2009
746.0463	£12.99

British Library CIP Data available
ISBN 978-086315-678-6
Printed in Singapore

Contents

Introduction 7

The History of Felting 9

Useful Facts about Wool 12
and Wool Suppliers

Where to get Wool for Felting 16

Setting up your Work Space 17

Preparing the Wool 18

About the Colours 21

Basic Instructions 24

Important Tips 31

Creative Possibilities 34

Making Felt with Children 40

The Story of the Sheepdog and 46
the Lamb

Hats 48
Black-brown beret 48
Violet beret 48
Boy's hat with a feather 49
Purple hat with grape decoration 51

Jewellery 52
Oak leaf pin brooch 52
Cherry pin brooch 52
Grape pin brooch 52
Orange necklace 53
Necklace with shell 53
Felt setting for semi — precious 53
stone
Hair slide 54
Violet necklace 54
Friendship rings 54
Heart and flower necklaces 55

For Cold Feet 57
Hot water bottle cover 57
Insoles 57
Mushroom slippers 59
Woollen boots 60

Beautiful Gift-wrap 63
Pouches 63
Party bag with red dots and 64
satin ribbon
Large felt bag with colourful stars 65
Large envelope 66

Felted Things for a Baby	68
Rattle ball	68
Teething ring	68
Bottle warmer	69
Covers to Protect and Decorate	70
Recorder cases	70
Glasses cases	71
Book covers	72
Treasure bags	73
Dolls	75
Sack doll	75
Doll with arms and legs	79
Small doll in a sleeping bag	80
Beautiful things for dolls	83
'Birth of a doll'	85
Seasonal Toys — Spring	86
Spring fairy	86
Easter eggs	91
Five small rabbits	92
Easter nests	94
Large rabbit	95
Seasonal Toys — Summer	100
Magic flower and flower child	100
Felted vegetables	103
Butterflies	105
Seasonal Toys — Autumn	106
Mushroom gnome	106
Leaf bag	108
Seasonal Toys — Winter	110
Star music box	110
Santa Claus boot	111
Hollow Christmas tree	113
Igloo	115
Inuit dolls	116
Polar bears	119
Dressing up	122
Dog hat	123
Rabbit hat	126
Cockerel	128
More ideas	130
Juggling balls	131
Gnomes	131
Tiny swaddled dolls	132
Hand puppet	133
Finger puppets	136
Heart bags	139
Teddy bear	142
Fried eggs	149
Fish music box	149
Fleece shawl	152

Introduction

There are several factors that make felting a truly fascinating craft. Firstly, there is the actual material, the wool. Unlike any other substance, wool is able to change from a light, fluffy mass into a stable, long-lasting fabric full of practical uses. All that is needed is moisture, heat and pressure. Skilled hands can shape wool into beautiful and original objects — a truly magical material!

The second interesting factor is the history of the felting technique, dating back to ancient times. Hand felting was never, and is still not, dependent on technological inventions or developments. It remains exactly the same skill as it was over 3000 years ago. Success is dependent purely on skilful hands, a joy in experimenting and a feeling for form. Even if you have never touched a sewing needle, never mind a spindle or weaving shuttle, you can hand felt; this is the textile-making technique that preceded all others. Despite its age, hand felting has not become a major part of our cultural heritage, and so it has not been restricted or influenced by tradition or dogmas. This not only enables a fresh, creative approach to felting, but also requires us to work sensitively in this ancient craft. In practical terms, we should felt the wool into complete, seamless forms to make functional, useful objects. Cutting the felt into shape and then sewing it together should remain an exception. In general, scissors should only be used sparingly.

You will find a wide range of attractive and interesting things to felt in this book: hats, bags, rings, magic flowers, fish, igloos, dolls, gnomes and much more. There are both functional items to give as gifts and unique toys for children of all ages.

Differing levels of expertise are needed for these projects. The instructions are aimed at parents, grandparents, godparents and teachers who are interested in creative crafts and want to make unusual, individual things for their children. Some of these projects are also suitable for school age children to make, either on their own or with a little adult help.

Once you have learned the ancient technique of felting, you will become hooked; the range of possibilities are endless and the sense of achievement is great!

The bees and the sheep

"Is there a greater benefactor to humans among the animals than us?" the bees asked the human beings.

"Yes indeed," the humans replied.

"Which ones?"

"Sheep! Sheep's wool is necessary for our survival, while your honey is only a pleasant supplement. And do you not want to know another reason why I think the sheep is a greater benefactor than you, bee? The sheep gives me its wool without resistance; while I fear your sting when receiving honey."

Gotthold Ephraim Lessing: Fables, Book 3

The History of Felting

According to legend, Saint Clemens discovered the process of felting. He padded his shoes with some sheep's wool that a farmer had given him, and the friction, pressure, warmth and moisture soon transformed the wool into felt.

However, people used animal wool to make felt long before the time of Saint Clemens. It is possible to imagine what motivated the ancient hunters and gatherers to make felt themselves: observing the matting (felting) process in their own hair, or the process which occurred as a result of pressure, moisture and warmth on the animal hairs they gathered to make themselves a soft bed. One thing is certain: people have known about the excellent quality of wool for a long time, otherwise they would not have domesticated wild mountain sheep. Later, through breeding and selection, the Romans created the foundations of all the different races and sub-species of sheep that we know today. The Romans not only wore fine, natural white woollen togas, but also hand felted hats.

Many different tribes throughout the world used felting as an ancient technique to make material. Not much was needed: two hands, a good eye and some feeling for form were sufficient. Over time, different production methods developed, depending on the skill and needs of the people. In particular, the nomads of the Asian Steppes proved that it is possible to use wool to felt almost any shape imaginable. Their lives have been intertwined with felting for thousands of years, and a surprising variety of felted objects have evolved, which range from roofs for their mobile round houses, called yurts, to pieces of clothing, saddlebags and yoghurt warmers.

The large, usually trapeze-shaped, roof felt mats of the yurts are produced communally. The freshly shorn wool is beaten and then spread evenly on a mat of straw or reeds. The wool is sprinkled with water and rolled up within the mats. With the help of ropes this roll is moved back and forth, turned round, watered for hours and then unrolled again. This produces an incredibly strong roof felt, a reliable protection from the elements. The roof mats above the entranceway of yurts are often decorated with skilful embroidery, ornaments and traditional magic symbols. When the Nomads move on to pastures new, they only have to fold up the yurt's skeleton walls and roll up the roofs.

Buddhist monks belonging to the Uighur tribe in China still produce beautiful, simple felted carpets according to their ancient tradition. The wool of twenty sheep is needed for one carpet. First they beat the wool to loosen it and remove

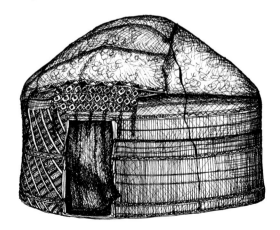

Afghan yurt. Often the curly texture of the sheep's wool can still be seen on its felted roof.

any dirt, then they spread it out evenly on a large bamboo mat. After wetting it, they roll it up. In the blistering heat, two monks rotate the roll with their bare feet to the rhythms of ritual singing until a solid felt sheet has been produced.

Archaeologists found the mummified body of a woman in an oasis in the Taklamakan Desert, probably dating from the Chinese Han Dynasty. Her head was protected by a felt hat, decorated with two heron feathers. Her shoes were made from camel leather.

The felting techniques of some indigenous tribes in Peru are also of particular interest.

Peru has the largest number of sheep of all the Andean countries. The extreme mountain climate near the Equator prompted the inhabitants to make protective headgear. Even today they felt beautiful, imaginative hats in unusual shapes — flat hats, melon-shaped hats, caps, sombreros etc. The women often pin these quite large structures to their thick plaits with long needles. The hats are usually richly and colourfully embroidered. Some are also decorated with tassels and small, punched out pieces of metal foil.

The oldest preserved felt objects are in the Hermitage in St Petersburg. Among other things

Mongolian yurt

there are small, stylised swans made out of white felt, stuffed with straw. They date back approximately 2500 years, and were used for cult purposes as part of the burial ritual of a Scythian ruler.

It has been reported that in some Russian provinces thick, solid boots were hand felted as recently as fifty years ago. They were so warm they could be worn outside in winter, and then dried over the stove at night.

As these short tales show, the art of felting has only been preserved in a few remote regions of the world. It has long been forgotten in our society.

Hand felting was rediscovered in the seventies, when various artists in the USA, Eastern Europe, Holland and Germany started to look for other creative methods of making textiles. Initially, they worked independently from one another, experimenting with this fascinating technique. Soon they offered felting courses, and the skills they had acquired were then passed on to people interested in learning about ancient textile techniques.

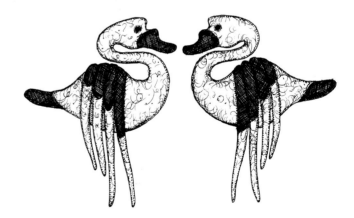

Indigenous Peruvian woman wearing a hand felted, richy embroidered flat-topped hat with attached cloth

Felt hat found in a grave in the Taklaman desert

These small felt swans look very modern, but they date back approximately 2,500 years. They were once part of the burial ceremony of a Scythian ruler and were filled with straw.

Useful Facts about Wool and Wool Suppliers

Why does wool felt?

When still on the animal wool does not felt as the fibres all grow in the same direction, and a greasy secretion surrounding each fibre prevents them from becoming tangled. But once the sheep has been shorn, the fibres loose their parallel structure and become 'chaotic'. When the wool is moistened with warm water, the scales splay out from the stem of the fibre and expand. Friction and pressure make the fibres swim around each other and then twist, tangle and interlock together. Adding an alkaline product supports this process. Once the wool cools down, the scales constrict again, resulting in a more or less compact mass of wool — the felt.

Sheep's wool

Sheep's wool is one of the oldest and most widely used textile fibres in the world. Like all other animal fibres, it consists of the protein keratin. Each fibre grows out of a hair follicle which is richly supplied with blood. On average, a sheep has 10,000 follicles per square centimetre of skin. The fibre grows about 0.2 mm a day.

Seen under a microscope, the wool fibres show a distinct scale-like structure. These scales overlap like roof tiles and surround the wool fibre. The 'inside' of a fibre consists of crimped, highly elastic cells (fibrils). The scales are layered towards the tip of the fibre and have an open

Different natural shades of raw wool

structure. The fibres absorb moisture and dirt and prevent them from reaching the skin. A fully-grown sheep's fleece, carefully parted, reveals the clean, pink skin of the sheep as well as the beautiful natural white wool. Tiny golden droplets of lanolin glisten in the wool and help protect the animal's skin. Towards the middle the wool traps small particles of dirt, while coarser dirt, burs and pieces of straw are caught on the outside.

The composition and amount of scales surrounding the wool fibre is of prime importance for felting. The more scales there are, the better the wool felts. This differs from sheep to sheep.

Among others, New Zealand and Friesian milk sheep, and their crossbreeds, offer the best results. The wool from Bavarian mountain sheep, Wurttemberg country sheep and blackface sheep can also be used. Pure merino wool felts quickly and gives a loose, voluminous mat. Long, hard, straight wool, for example from a German moorland sheep, is less effective. It is possible to create interesting structures with long straight wool if there is sufficient underwool to felt it together.

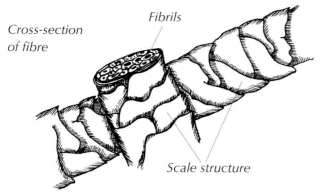

Cross-section of fibre

Fibrils

Scale structure

Wool fibres seen under a microscope. The scale structure is clearly visible and is of great importance for felting.

The quality of, and ability to, felt is not only dependent on the breed of sheep. Other factors include the health of the animal, its diet, age and the climate it was subjected to, as well as the grease content of the wool, the amount of dirt, as well as the fleece's storage conditions and length of storage.

Beautiful, durable felt can also be made with animal hair that does not felt well, and even plant fibres and silk can be used if mixed with suitable felting wool. Natural coloured, not too greasy wool felts best. Dyed wool is sometimes more difficult to felt, as the mordanting and dyeing process can damage the scales surrounding the wool fibre. Although this means the wool looses some of its felting capacity, it can still be successfully felted onto a natural coloured wool fleece.

Alpaca

Alpacas belong to the camel family native to the countries of the Andes. Their black-brown coloured wool is particularly high quality. Glossiness, silkiness, fibre length and the beautiful natural colours make it an attractive choice for the felter. Alpaca wool felts more slowly than sheep's wool, but it is worth the extra effort as the result is a light felt with a silky sheen.

Camel hair

Camel hair only felts satisfactorily if it does not contain too many kemp hairs. These long, wiry hairs are not crinkled at all and only have a few large scales surrounding the wool fibre. But underwool and baby camel hair felts quite well. When mixed half and half with sheep's wool it makes a beautiful felt. Choose similarly coloured sheep's wool to maintain the warm camel hair colour. You can also combine baby camel hair with schappe silk or cashmere to produce very fine material.

Alpaca roving (top left) and camel hair (bottom left); baby camel and dog hair (top right front and back); mohair (centre right) and carded sheep's wool (bottom right)

13

Cashmere

Cashmere is the wool 'closest to heaven.' The small, frugal Cashmere goat resides in the sparse high plateaus of Asia. The underwool, called cashmere down, is particularly popular. It is fine, dense, clean and indescribably soft. Cashmere is good for felting. In the past, Chinese people made hats out of cashmere down to protect themselves against the raw winds of the highlands.

Cashmere is far too valuable to be felted by itself, but carded together with a fine sheep's wool or as a thin outer layer on wool, it makes a gorgeous piece of material. You can then brush the cashmere product to give it a fluffy, beautiful surface, as the Chinese used to do.

Cashmere (top left), Angora rabbit (top right), plant-dyed silk wool (bottom)

Mohair

The Angora goat originates from the Asian part of Turkey. Its name derives from the old trading town of Angora. Its snow-white fleece is extremely silky and lustrous. The long fibres are particularly durable, but only have a few, weakly developed scales. Because of this they do not felt well. Combined with wool that felts well and then brushed, it produces lustrous, longhaired mohair felt (see 'Sack doll' page 75).

Angora

Real Angora wool does not come from the Angora goat, as one might imagine, but from a rabbit. This snow-white animal used to be called the 'English silk rabbit.' It is a pleasant, patient and very tame pet, which can be shorn every three months. A well-kept rabbit can yield up to one kilo of wool a year.

Besides its healing properties for joint and muscle diseases, it also has other highly valued qualities — it only weighs a third of a comparable piece of sheep's wool but has the same warmth capacity. Even sensitive skin is not irritated by Angora wool.

Angora wool is suitable for felting, but it takes twice as long to felt as sheep's wool. Because of this, it is better to card it together with, or felt it onto, a layer of sheep's wool. Always felt the sheep's wool side first.

Felting Angora rabbit wool is a slippery affair, but the result is well worth the effort. The soft, fluffy surface becomes even more beautiful if brushed once dry (see 'Glasses cases' page 71, 'Berets' page 48).

Dog hair

If you own a dog you can make a piece of trial felt out of brushed or shorn hairs. Most dog hair, more precisely the underneath hair, felts surprisingly well. The pungent smell of 'wet dog' disappears after felting. Dog hair is also suitable for combining with other fibres, for example alpaca. The black-brown coloured treasure bag on page 73 was felted using only dog hair, the beret on page 48 was made with one third dog hair. In this case, the hair of a longhaired mongrel was brushed out and collected for several months. Felt made from dog hair is very solid.

Silk

During its short life the silkworm undergoes a complete metamorphosis: from an egg to a caterpillar, from a caterpillar to a cocoon, from a cocoon to a moth. Silk is very sleek as well as dirt and damp resistant. Its shine and gloss mean it has a special place among natural fibres. There was a time when only the Chinese emperors were allowed to wear silk garments.

In contrast to wool, silk does not have a cell structure, but it can be carded with all other felt friendly materials, or felted as a thin layer on top, which allows us to profit from its wonderful texture. We use the silk wool made from silk waste and cut up cocoons, called *schappe*. *Tussah-schappe* silk mixtures are also suitable. Silk dyes excellently with plant dyes. The red glasses case on page 71 has a thin inner layer of silk felted to the red wool.

Chemically dyed wool roving (left) and hand crafted, plant dyed magic wool (right)

Where to Get Wool for Felting

All the fibres described above can be obtained from craft shops. Almost all are suitable for felting. Prepared, machine carded wool, called wool *roving* or *tops*, has already been optimally prepared for felting; it has been washed, cleaned and carded, and is particularly suitable for beginners. Wool roving is available in many bright colours. It is made out of long staple, high-quality wool and is also suitable for spinning. The wool has been carded to align the fibres and produce a long, continuous cord. Felt made out of roving is even and smooth with an opaque sheen. Roving is good for making even striped patterns and long, strong cords. The long fibres also make it suitable for 'drawing.' Dip the fibres into warm water and use them like a brush stroke to 'paint' wavy lines, feathers, petals, outlines etc.

Wide fleece *batts* are easy to work with, and are usually slightly cheaper, as they contain short fibres that are less suited to spinning. They are large carded mats of wool made out of thin, well-connected layers. Wool batts are used for making large areas of felt and particularly for modelling and constructing three-dimensional figures, as it is easy to separate off the exact amount of wool required. They often contain small burrs. Remove them before you start, as they can rub the skin off your water-softened hands while felting.

Greasy wool straight from the fleece has to be washed, teased and carded before it can be felted. If you know a local farmer nearby, you may be able to buy a freshly shorn fleece. Shearing occurs around the beginning of May.

Ask the farmer for a fleece from an animal which has been shorn for the second time in its life, as this second shearing is said to be the best!

Setting up your Work Space

A large, stable table with a waterproof top is suitable for felting and fulling. Make sure there is a source of hot water — a kettle or stove — as well as a sink nearby. The floor should also be water resistant. A kitchen or large bathroom is usually the best place. In summer, if the weather is good, you can work outside. You will need to take a bucket of hot water out with you.

You will also need a *felting board*, which is technically known as a *fulling board*. These can be bought from spinning wheel or wool suppliers. Before buying a felting board, ask your friends and family if they have an old unused washboard in their cellar or attic, or look out for one at a flea market — they can be used just as effectively. In an emergency, you can also use a grooved draining board.

All other equipment is made up of everyday household items: a one litre container, scissors, lead pencil, towel, needle and thread, bucket, a cloth for wiping, a box for the templates and hand cream.

Soap is an important medium. Its alkaline components make the scales of the wool fibre open up, considerably accelerating the felting process. The soap also enables your hands to glide over the work piece, ensuring an even felt with a beautiful surface. All good quality curd soaps or curd flakes are suitable. I myself work solely with Marseille olive oil soap (600 g block, from health food stores), as it moisturises the skin and neither dries out the wool nor the hands. Many felters prefer working with soft soap or

Items needed for felting

detergents. Whisk approximately one tablespoon of soft soap into one litre of lukewarm water.

You can either scatter soap shavings directly over wet wool, or dissolve the soap in warm water so that there are no lumps of soap in the felt. To do this, place the soap square into a shallow dish, for example a soup bowl, and sprinkle warm water over it now and again. A thick, creamy soap will collect in the base. Depending on the amount required, take some of the creamy soap with your fingertips and place it directly onto the wool, or run your hand or the wool over the bar of soap. Ultimately, the type of soap and how to use it is your personal choice.

If you purchase your wool directly from a farmer, you will need a pair of *hand carders* (see page 19) to make even wool roving suitable for felting Hand carders are also indispensable for anyone wanting to experiment with mixing different fibres and colours.

It is only worth buying a *drum carder* (see page 20) once felting has turned into a serious hobby. Carding machines come with a crank handle or an electric motor.

Preparing the Wool

Sorting

First, unroll the fleece onto the floor. If the sheep shearer has done a good job, the fleece will be in the shape of the sheep with its legs spread out. The leg wool and the wool around the tail are usually full of droppings, and can thus be discarded. Often the wool from the stomach is also unusable. Cut off the tips of the wool which are yellowed or singed by the sun and remove any pieces of plants. To finish, firmly shake out the fleece — a considerable amount of dirt will still fall out. Now it is ready to wash.

Washing

Soak the fleece overnight in plenty of cool water. The ability of wool to clean itself is impressive, as you will see the next morning when the dirt flushes out in waves. Then wash the wool in clean, lukewarm water, using the same soap as recommended for felting, to remove part of the wool grease. Shave off flakes of soap and add them to the water. A brew made from the soapbark tree also produces a good result. After washing the wool once, make a sample piece of felt. If it still feels greasy and is difficult to felt, then repeat the washing process again. To finish, rinse the wool three times with clean water and dry it in a shady place.

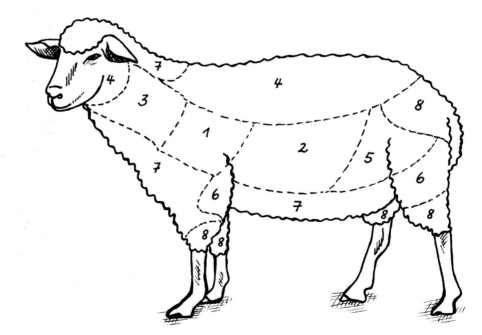

The different qualities of a sheep's fleece. 1 refers to the highest, 8 to the lowest quality wool.

18

Important: Be very careful while washing and rinsing. Do not rub or wring out the wool. The washing and rinse water should be the same temperature, 30°C (86°F) at maximum. It will not harm the wool to gently spin it in a washing machine after the last rinse.

Teasing

The carefully washed and dried wool should now be workable and pliable with a silky finish. It should also smell very pleasant. Friends and family can now all join in the teasing process. Teasing should be done with care; do not tug or tear at the wool. Take a lock of wool and hold it between the ball of the thumb and the rest of the fingers of both hands. Then carefully pull it apart at right angles to the fibre direction. This is called 'opening.' Sort the teased wool into piles according to their quality while you work. It is not necessary to card well-teased wool, as the curly structure can give an interesting felting pattern. Opening and teasing wool also removes any remaining dirt particles.

Carding

Working with a pair of *hand carders* constitutes the basis of *carding.* Each carder consists of an oblong piece of wood with a thick piece of leather fixed to one side. Small metal teeth, bent towards the handle, stick out of the leather.

Spread out the carefully teased wool onto one carder. Hold this carder in your left hand (or right if you are left-handed) and place it on your left thigh with the handle pointing outwards. Take the other, empty carder in your right hand. Stretch out your right forefinger onto the back of the carder. The teeth should be pointing in opposite directions. Gently brush over the first carder with the empty carder from left to right. Do not pull the carders obliquely over one another. Make sure the teeth do not touch and get caught up in each other while carding.

Once the wool has transferred to the second (right) carder, turn both carders so that their handles and teeth are facing in the same direction.

Working with hand carders

19

A few sweeping movements loosens the wool, and it comes off as a *rolag*. This rolag can then be transferred to the left carder again and the procedure repeated from the start.

High quality, well-teased wool often only needs carding once to make it suitable for felting. Colour or fibre mixtures need to be carded two or three times. A few last remaining dirt particles will still fall out of the wool while carding.

Carding with a drum carder

Using a drum carder with a manual handle allows for carding larger amounts of wool in a shorter time. It is excellent for thoroughly mixing different kinds of fibres or colours. The machine consists of two rollers, a larger and a smaller one. Both rollers are covered in little teeth that point in opposite directions, and do not touch one another when turned. The rollers are connected by a drive belt. Place a handful of well-teased wool onto the slat in front of the smaller roller. The teeth will grasp the wool when you turn the handle in a clockwise direction. The fibres are pulled under the roller and stretched, until the teeth of the larger roller grasp them. The actual carding process takes place between the two rollers. Continue feeding small portions of teased wool onto the slat, spreading it out evenly across the width of the roller, while slowly turning the handle. Soon an even band of carded wool will surround the larger roller. You can loosen the wool along the seam of the carding cloth, where there are no teeth. Push a long screwdriver or similar implement under the wool. Carefully manoeuvre the wool from the teeth and lift it off the roller while trying to keep the fleece as intact as possible.

Drum carder

About the Colours

The objects depicted in this book are all either a natural wool colour — as obtained from the animal — or plant-dyed wool. Purple and pink coloured wool are dyed using cochineal, from the cochineal beetle bred on the Canary Islands.

Use the precious plant-dyed wool sparingly. Sometimes a coloured accent suffices (red cochineal dots on a natural white background, see 'Gift bag' page 63). Often plant-dyed wool is only used for the outer layer to make a coloured surface, like a 'gold leaf covering,' for example, the shoes on page 60. A white inner layer, particularly for shoes, also looks attractive.

You can buy chemically dyed wool roving in many shades. So-called *magic wool* — plant-dyed, unspun sheep's wool — can be bought in specialist craft shops. Larger amounts of plant-dyed, unspun sheep's wool should be bought directly from felting workshops. Ask whether the wool has been dyed gently and slowly without poisonous mordants (colour fixing agents).

If you want to try your hand at dyeing, you can use chemical textile colours (batik colours) as well as natural pigments. Follow the instructions on the packet.

Dyeing with plants

Dyeing with plants was seen as a magic art in the Middle Ages. Plant pigments penetrate deeply into the fibres, giving a wonderful warmth, richness and depth of natural colour that can invoke a real sense of harmony; the whole colour spectrum resonates within each single colour. Chemical colour pigments are isolated and remain *on* the fibre, which gives them a harsher look.

Good examples of the durability of plant colours can be seen in ancient preserved materials, for example Coptic wall hangings from the fifth century, whose colours are still bright and fresh today.

Remember that plant dyeing at home requires a considerable amount of work, as well as the use of energy and water. If at all possible, only use plants which grow back quickly. Never use poisonous mordants like copper sulphate, tin (stannous chloride), iron (ferrous sulphate). Unfortunately, these mordants are still often recommended in the relevant literature.

Plants which grow in our latitude mainly give shades of yellow and brown. These vary depending on location and are influenced by the climate to which the plant is exposed. Time of harvest also plays a part. Even the mood of the dyer supposedly has an affect on the nuances and permanence of the colours. For the following recipes, well-known, easily found plants have been used.

Fixing the colour

The colour fixing process, which always precedes the actual dyeing, opens up the fibres and enables the plant juices to penetrate deeply into the wool fibres. This ensures luminosity and sets the colour. Colour fixing agents are called *mordants*.

Recipes for dyes

Red-brown from pine cones

1 kilo (2 lb) pine cones
100 g (3 $^1/_2$ oz) wool

Mordant
Dissolve 25 g alum and 25 g cream of tartar in a tub of cold water. Add the wool. Make sure there is sufficient water for the wool to float in. Bring everything to the boil, gently and frequently moving the wool. Simmer for an hour. Leave the wool in a cool place in the mordant liquid for one to two days, turning it over twice a day.

Dyeing
Collect pine cones from different conifers and chop them up. Cover them with water and soak them in a dye bath for one to two days. Boil them for an hour and then strain the liquid.

Place the 'mordant' wool into the prepared, cold pine-cone dye bath and gradually bring it back to the boil. Simmer for one hour, moving the wool around now and again. Let it cool down in the dye bath. Then rinse until the water runs clear.

Note: Even when rinsing, give the wool plenty of time. Let the wool rest for a while in the first rinsing water for the colour to bleed out. This saves a lot of rinsing water later.

Medium yellow from marigolds

1 kilo (2 lb) marigolds
100 g (3 $^1/_2$ oz) wool

Mordant
Use 50 g alum this time and prepare in the same way as described in the pine-cone recipe.

Dyeing
Boil the chopped up marigolds for an hour, let the dye bath cool and sieve. Then continue as the pine-cone recipe.

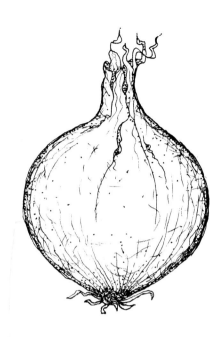

Green-yellow from apple-tree bark

500 g (1 lb) apple-tree bark
100 g (3 1/2 oz) wool

Ask a fruit farmer for twigs and branches after pruning in early spring. Chop up entire twigs and peel the bark from the branches of felled trees. Chop everything up and dry.

Mordant
Use 25 g alum and prepare in the same way as described in the pine-cone recipe.

Dyeing
Soak the apple-tree bark for two days, boil for three hours and strain. Simmer the wool in the dye bath for an hour.

Golden yellow from onion skins

200 g (7 oz) onion skins
100 g (3 1/2 oz) wool

Mordant
Use 20 g alum and 10 g cream of tartar and simmer in the mordant for an hour.

Dyeing
This time layer the 'mordant' wool and the onion skins in the dyeing pot, fill it with water and add a handful of copper pennies. Simmer for an hour. Let the wool cool down overnight in the dye bath.

Basic Instructions

Several steps are necessary to make a good piece of felt:

1. *Cutting out a template,* to give the shape or size;
2. *Spreading out the layers of wool* on or around the template;
3. The actual *felting* — rubbing and massaging the wool by hand with the help of warm water and soap;
4. *Fulling* over a ridged board (washboard, felting board, ridged draining board), which shrinks the material again substantially and can also influence the shape;
5. Thorough *rinsing* to remove the soapsuds.

Templates

All the templates used for making the objects in this book are made from cardboard — either from a cardboard box or the back of a sketch block. Corrugated cardboard is not suitable as it dissolves quickly. Make sure the cardboard does not bleed colour.

Remember when cutting the template that the wool shrinks during felting, therefore make it two to three centimetres larger all around than the intended finished size of the work piece. The cardboard needs to be thick enough for you to feel it through the layers of wool and to survive the strain of felting. After felting, the cardboard template has done its duty and has usually disintegrated. Because of this it is useful to keep a copy of each template for later use.

Spreading out the wool

Spreading out the wool over or around the template is an important step which determines the later quality of the felted object. This step should be carried out with great care.

For a flat felt sheet

To make a flat piece of felt, use the template solely for determining the size. Remember to make it slightly larger than the desired finished size. Divide the weighed wool into several equal portions and then spread even layers of wool over the template in thin layers. Place alternating layers at right angles to each other, with the fibre direction lying once horizontally, then once vertically (see figure 7.1). This gives the scales of the wool fibres more of a chance to interlock. Carefully smooth and spread the water outwards over the entire area. Then slowly and gently rub and stroke the wool, being careful not to push the wet wool over the edge of the template. Repeatedly smooth your hands along the wool at the edges of the template, working from the outside to the centre more often than vice versa. As the wool felts beneath your hands, massage and rub more strongly, until the felt reaches the desired thickness.

It is a good idea for beginners to start off with pieces of 'practice felt' to give them a feel for felting. It is also useful to have a collection of felt with different colours and thickness, for example to use as a patch for repairing a hole, for appliqué, for cutting out leaves, etc. These practice pieces allow you to experiment with the different kinds of fibres, find out the amount of shrinkage, or try out different patterns.

For shaped felt

It is surprising and exciting how many different shapes can be felted out of wool. You can make almost anything if you follow a few simple rules. Sketch the desired shape on cardboard. Round off any points or corners slightly. Cut out the template two to three centimetres larger than the desired finished piece, as this is the average shrinkage rate. However, shrinkage depends on several factors: individual work method, length and vigour of felting and fulling and the nature of the wool, for example, grease content, sheep breed etc.

How to felt

Wind the weighed, well-teased wool around the template in layers (see figures 7.2–7.4). Alternate the main direction of the fibres from layer to layer as much as possible. Wet each layer with warm water and press it down with a flat hand (figure 7.5). The water should be as hot as your hands can stand. Before laying down a new layer of wool, dry your hands well, as only dry, airy wool can be teased and spread out evenly. If you want a different colour for the inner layer of the felted piece, place it as the last layer over the template (figure 7.6). By the end of this process, you should have wound the wool firmly and evenly around the cardboard template. Wind the wool around the cardboard like a bandage; long fibred, well-carded wool is an advantage.

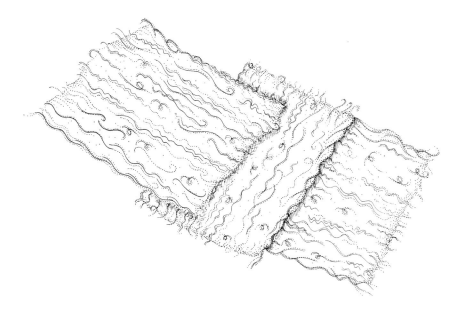

7.1 *As far as it is possible and visible, the layers of wool should be placed at right angles to each other, the main fibre direction lying once horizontally, once vertically over each other. This increases the durability of the later felt.*

The cardboard template is now *between* the layers of wool. It has two purposes: to give the felt its shape, and to prevent the layers from felting together. This means that a space has been created between the layers, which is necessary for making bags, hats etc.

Note: Place an extra layer of wool over any areas that will later be subject to stress and strain; for example, the soles, heels and toes of shoes, the lower and upper end of recorder cases and the lower edges of bags. Take particular care when felting difficult parts like curves, points and indentations; the wool layers can easily slip away in these areas as you wind them around the template, resulting in holes or thin patches.

Feel around the finished piece of felt thoroughly with your fingertips to check for any thin areas or holes and if necessary add an extra layer of wool.

Then tap and press the wet mass of wool against the template, moulding it well. Do not worry about later openings yet; the shaped felt piece is only cut open once it is stable enough.

7.3   *Wind wool around the template (horizontally)*

7.4   *Wind wool around the template (vertically)*

7.2   *Template with stripes for the pattern*

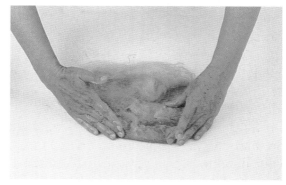

7.5   *Wet each layer*

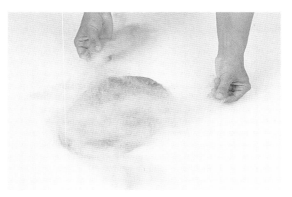

7.6 *White wool, the later inside colour, is placed around the template*

7.7 *Distributing the soap flakes*

Felting

Sprinkle soap flakes over the wet, prepared wool package (figure 7.7) and pour a small well of hot water in its centre. With soaped up hands, start rubbing from the centre outwards, very carefully and initially without much pressure. Your hands should glide easily over the wool. You can use the washboard as a base for small pieces of felt (figure 7.8). After only a few minutes you will feel the felting process starting to take place: the wool fibres begin to intertwine, the formerly soft piece solidifies more and more. The more stable the piece becomes — that is, felts — the more vigorously you have to rub, press and massage.

For a *flat piece of felt* (see page 24) the template is only used to determine the shape and size. The wool must not extend beyond its edges if you want to 'keep the shape.' For this reason, rub inwards from the edge of the template more often than the other way round and use the edge of your hand to repeatedly rub around the edges of the template.

When *felting a shape* it is important to clearly mould your desired shape. To do this, rub around the shape repeatedly, pressing the wool against the template (figure 7.8). Felt tight, fiddly parts and small curves with only two fingers.

If the wool is too dry with too little soap, single fibre strands will be rubbed upwards, resulting in a rough texture. If this happens, add more hot water and soap flakes.

Throughout the felting process, regularly press out the surplus, cooled water and add fresh

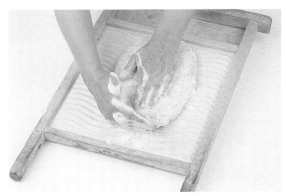

7.8 *Felting. Washboard as a base. Rub around the shape with your hands.*

27

hot water and more soap flakes. If the piece has already started to felt, it will do no harm to squeeze it out over the sink.

Note: Too much wetness and soap hinders the felting process, as the fibres liquify. For best results, the suds should be solid and white like whipped cream.

Fulling

Only start *fulling* once the piece has been well felted and the fibres are strongly interlocked. Fulling, the most vigorous step, allows the fibres to interlock even more tightly, which increases the material's stability and durability. The surface becomes firm and smooth.

The final shape of the object can still be influenced during this process, as the felt shrinks in the direction in which it is being fulled. Use this fact to your advantage when trying to make a hat fit properly, for example.

How to full

Immerse the piece of felt in hot water and gently squeeze out the surplus water. Scatter some soap flakes on the washboard or felting board, and vigorously rub the soaped piece of felt over it. It can either be flat, rolled or folded during this process, but make sure that the object is evenly fulled in all directions (figures 7.9 and 7.10). If the object will not be subjected to tough treatment later on, you do not need to full it. Shoes, hats and bags should always be fulled.

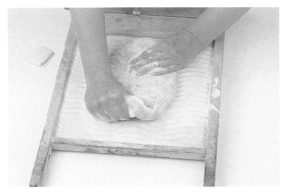

7.9   *Fulling*

7.10

7.11   *The finished piece lifts off the base completely when testing the felt*

7.12 *Cutting the felt open*

7.13 *Removing the template*

7.14 *Felting and fulling the inside*

7.15

7.16

Only cut an opening in a piece of shaped felt (figure 7.12) once you have successfully performed the felting test (see figure 7.11 and the diagram of the felting test, figures 7.17 and 7.18).

Remove the used, wet template (figure 7.13). Turn the whole piece of felt inside out and vigorously felt and full the inside (figures 7.14–7.16). Felt the cut edges particularly well to make them less obvious, using plenty of soap.

29

Felting test

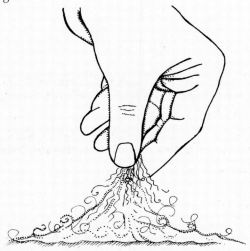

7.17 *If single fibres can be pulled out of the felt and the piece cannot be lifted off the base as a whole, then you have to continue felting*

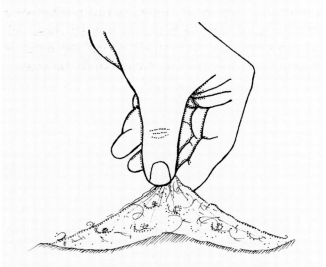

7.18 *The flet is finished once it can be completely lifted off the base using the thumb and forefinger, without too many single fibres coming loose*

7.19 *Two felted and rinsed bags made from one template*

Rinsing

Soap needs to be rinsed out thoroughly to stop the fibres becoming damaged. Rinse and wring the finished felt product three times in clear water, adding a shot of vinegar to the last rinsing bath. Most pieces can then be spun in a washing machine. To finish, press and knead the object into shape and let it dry on a towel. Modelled animals, for example the polar bear and the large rabbit (pages 95 and 119), should only be showered to rinse. Never ring them out or spin them in a washing machine.

Important Tips

If something goes wrong, don't give up — there is usually a remedy.

Testing the felt

Grasp the felt between your thumb and forefinger. It should lift up completely from the background (see figures 7.17 and 7.18). If too many single fibres come loose then you need to continue felting.

Scissors

A pair of scissors is indispensable for cutting openings and slits into shaped felt. You will also need them to cut out small leaves etc. for decorations or to trim the brim of a hat.

It is worth thinking about whether a picture needs to be cut exactly square, or if the edge of a bag really does look better cut completely straight. Visible traces of our felting handiwork and shapes that have been developed organically from the technique can often make the piece more interesting and add character.

If you have to cut an edge, round it off or re-felt it to ensure it does not look sharp-edged.

Holes or thin areas

These usually occur for one of two reasons:
1. The wool was not evenly distributed at the beginning.
2. There was too much vigorous rubbing at the start of felting, leading to the felt layers slipping apart.

What to do

If you notice the flaw before the felting process is too far advanced, place some additional wool onto the affected areas. It will still reliably felt into the rest.

However, once the felting process is finished, there are no 'hooks' left to grasp new wool. So this area needs to be fixed with a patch: sew on a matching, separately felted 'wool plaster' or a thin piece of sample felt with tiny stitches. Felt over this bit again vigorously. Often the patch is incorporated so well that it can hardly be seen.

Bulging edges on a shaped piece of felt

This is a common mistake that occurs when the wool extends beyond the edge of the template while felting, meaning that the cardboard cannot keep the layers of wool separated at that point, and they felt together.

What to do
Make sure the wet wool stays well pressed against the edge of the template right from the start, and rub around the edges often with the edge of your hand. Once the bulge is established, though, accept it as a 'coincidental design feature.' Small or still loose bulges can still be smoothed out: remove the template, flatten the bulge and vigorously felt and full the area.

Shapeless, holey 'pancake'

This means the wool was rubbed over the edges of the template, and the centre became thinner and thinner. So 'discipline' the wool — rub around the shape repeatedly, pushing back the wool. With circular movements, work from the outside to the inside more often than vice versa, and do not start fulling too early!

Soft edges

In this case, the object was not felted evenly. Places that are awkward to felt are often neglected, for example, edges, corners, curves and indentations.

Strands of surface felt have become loose

This can happen if you started rubbing too vigorously too soon and/or did not use enough soap. If the area is not too large, simply trim off these strands. Or you can sew them in place with a needle and thread. In both cases, re-felt these parts. You can also cover the area with a very thin new layer of wool and felt it on extremely carefully.

The whole piece of felt is loose and soft

1. It could be the type of wool.
2. The wool was not pressed down sufficiently after wetting, so not all the layers received water, and too much air remained between them. This means they could not felt together sufficiently.
3. As the felting process progressed, the object was not felted rigorously enough.

What to do
Wet everything again with hot water and felt.

Lopsided piece of felt

The wool always shrinks in the direction in which it is felted and fulled. A sheet of felt that has been primarily rubbed in its centre — where it is easiest — becomes 'waisted.'

What to do
Felt and full in all directions, particularly those where the object still needs to shrink.

The felt pattern is not sufficiently connected to the base layer

Sew the pattern on with tiny stitches and re-felt. This happens when either the pattern felt was felted too much and so could not connect to the wool base, or you stopped felting the whole piece too soon, before the pieces could join together sufficiently.

The felting process seems to be taking a long time

1. The material used does not have much natural felting ability.
2. You are working too tentatively the whole time — which is only necessary at the start!
3. The fibres are saturated in cold, watery 'soap sludge.'

What to do
Squeeze out the cold water and continue boldly with less water and more soapy lather. I hear 'This is never going to work!' in every felting course I run, and it has been disproved every time!

It can be discouraging for a beginner to find their wet shoes hanging off their feet, or a hat flopping right down to their chin. But at this stage, shortly after removing the template, there is no reason to be concerned. Continue working bravely and 'it will still turn into a shoe!'

Creative Possibilities

The following examples show further imaginative possibilities. Use them as inspiration for your own creativity:

- Felting small balls
- Marbled felt
- Mixing colours
- Checked felt
- Dots
- Painting with fibres
- Felting a fringe
- Appliqué
- Embroidering, quilting felt

Felting small balls

Different sized felt balls are always useful, e.g. for felted jewellery, necklaces, cherries, grapes, dolls' heads and buttons.

How to make them

Balls can be used for making dolls' heads, fruit, buttons and jewellery, among other things. Wind together a small, tight ball of wool and then wind thin layers of wool around it; dip it in warm soapy water and roll carefully between your hands. You can wind different coloured layers, which looks pretty if you are going to cut the ball in half after felting.

See 'Spring fairy' page 86 and 'Melons' page 104.

For more solid, sturdy balls, add the finished ball to a 40°C (100°F) or 60°C (140°F) washing machine cycle; knot them in a cotton sock to prevent them getting tangled with other items. If you want to make a barrel, egg or cone shape, first felt a ball and then firmly roll into the desired shape between your palms.

Marbled felt

Place a different coloured piece of teased wool, or several colours, in a very thin layer on top of the last layer.

See 'Book cover with star' page 72, 'White recorder cover' page 70 and rattle ball page 68.

Mixing colours

Wind one colour around the template, and then place a different coloured, evenly spread out thin layer on top; when felted the two colours will mix together to give a combination of both colours. This new colour will only become visible when you have been felting for some time and the lower layer evenly shines through. To make soft pastel colours, place a thin layer of white wool over the lower, coloured layer.

See 'Sack doll' page 75. A red wool layer was placed below the outer white layer, leading to a delicate rose colour.

Checked felt

Arrange thin strands of wool yarn (not 'superwash' yarns) in a checked pattern on or around the template. Place the layers of wool on top, and felt!

See 'Book cover' page 72 and 'Recorder cover' page 70.

Dotted pattern

Roll up small fluffs of wet wool between your thumb and forefinger. 'Stick' them to the template, place the layers of wool on top and felt.

See 'White gift bag' page 65, 'Felt pictures' page 41, 'Mushroom slippers' page 59.

Painting with fibres

You can 'paint' with fibres almost like with a brush. Long staple wool is best suited to this. Completely wet the fibres. Place them in any shape desired, letting them flow like paintbrush strokes. You can draw your pattern onto the template first. Once everything has been 'painted' — that is, placed on the template — spread out a layer of wool on top

Always felt from the back first to ensure the picture does not slip. See full instructions in figures 9.1–9.6 and 'Felt pictures' page 41, 'Large felt bag with colourful stars' page 65, 'Bookmark' page 43 and 'Hot water bottle cover' page 57.

9.2 *Place the flower face down on the cardboard and add stem and leaves*

9.3 *Cover the entire template with blue wool then cover with a white layer of wool*

9.1 *The petals were made with U-shaped small loops*

9.4 *Pour warm water into the centre, carefully rub and press with soapy hands*

9.5 *After about 20 minutes felting, carefully turn the picture over*

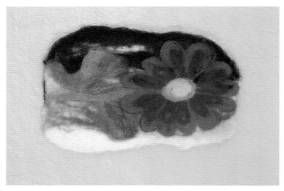

9.6 *Finished!*

Felt cords

Coloured felt cords can be used for making jewellery, plaiting, appliqué, dolls' hair and more. It is best to use wool roving or other long fibre wool.

If you only have short fibre wool available, carefully roll the short strands into a long cord, then wet and initially felt extremely gently. Knead the wet, soapy strand of wool centimetre by centimetre, rolling it slightly. Carefully pull it through your fist several times. Then place it on a wet towel and roll it back and forth under your flat hands, until the cord is strong and sturdy.

Felting a fringe

Let long strands of wool yarn (not 'superwash' yarns) hang out between the layers of felting wool where you want the fringe to be. The yarn will felt in well.

See 'Bookmark' page 43 and 'Doll's rug' page 43.

Modelled felt

To make an animal or other three-dimensional object, you will need to model and felt the wool. This process requires some skill and a good feeling for shapes and is not suitable for felting beginners. You will not need a template and rarely a sewing needle and thread. The body is freely constructed layer by layer using fleece batts, almost like modelling with clay. A tightly rolled up piece of fleece comprises the centre; everything else is added on, spread over, layered and carefully felted until the figure is finished. Once felted, the objects are very hardy and keep their shape well. Smaller figures with bendable arms and legs have wires inside their body, surrounded by tufts of wool which are then felted.

See 'Large rabbit' page 95 and 'Polar bear' page 119 for step-by-step instructions and illustrations.

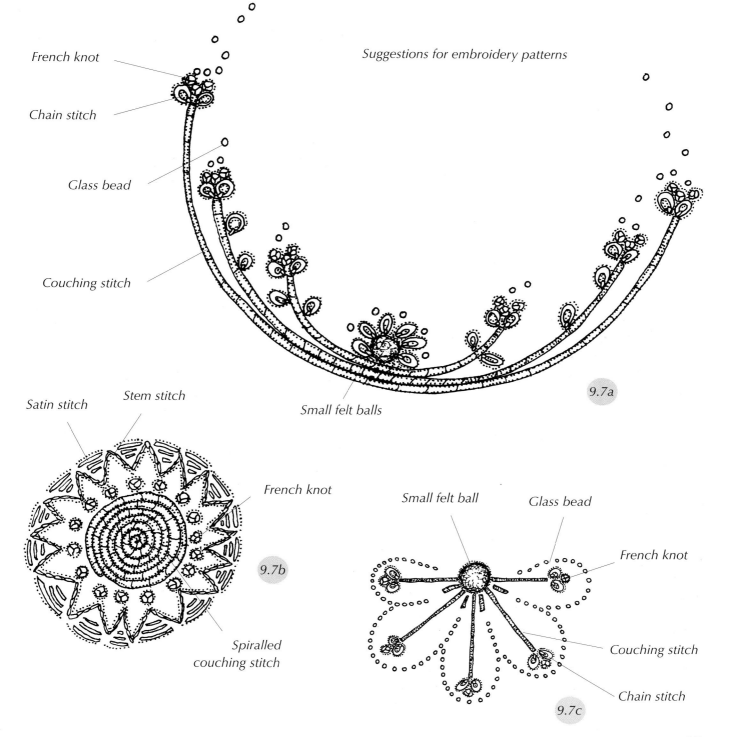

French knot

Chain stitch

Glass bead

Couching stitch

Suggestions for embroidery patterns

Small felt balls

9.7a

Satin stitch

Stem stitch

French knot

Spiralled
couching stitch

9.7b

Small felt ball

Glass bead

French knot

Couching stitch

Chain stitch

9.7c

37

Appliqué

Sew thin, cut-out felt shapes to the finished piece of felt with small, nearly invisible stitches. Then felt over the area again.

Note: Only thin felt appliqués merge well into the background. Thick shapes look clumsy.

See star on the 'Book cover' page 72.

Embroidering and quilting

A felted base is perfect for embroidering. You can let your imagination run wild, like the Peruvian women when decorating their hats. Beads, silk and metallic threads, or anything else you like can be used. Cut-out felt leaves look very three dimensional if you sew the leaf veins firmly with sewing silk and backstitch.

See 'Treasure bags' page 73 and 'Jewellery' page 52.

Using the same stitch, you can also make a checked quilted pattern over a larger area.

Different stitches for embroidering on felt

1. Satin stitch

It is important that the straight stitches lie evenly and closely together. Stagger the stitches when embroidering several rows, e.g. for doll's hair, place each new stitch between two stitches of the row before.

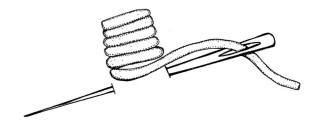

2. Stem stitch

Make sure the stitches are regular and fit snugly together. This stitch is good for embroidering fine lines or outlines. Two rows of stem stitch beside each other, sewn once from the right and once from the left, give a plait pattern.

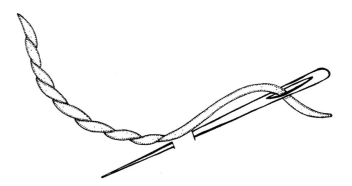

3. Chain stitch

Simple chain stitch can be used for many things: leaves, lines, borders, etc. Bring the needle up through the fabric. Make sure the thread always remains beneath the needle, and insert the needle back into the fabric where it first came out.

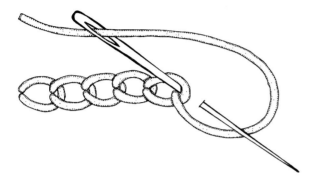

4. French knot

A French knot looks particularly decorative on felt. It is indispensable for floral designs and scattered patterns. As shown in the diagram, bring the needle out through the fabric and, keeping the thread taut and flat to the fabric, twist it around the needle.

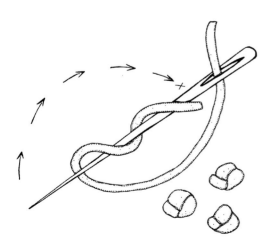

Then insert the needle back into the fabric vertically just beside the point from where it emerged. One twist is enough to make small knots; a larger knot requires two or more twists.

5. Couching stitch

You can make very pretty patterns with this embroidery technique. Lay thick lengths of wool or silk yarn in patterns on top of the felt, and then tack over it with sewing silk, thus anchoring it to the fabric.

See 'Treasure bags' page 73 and 'Red glasses case' page 71.

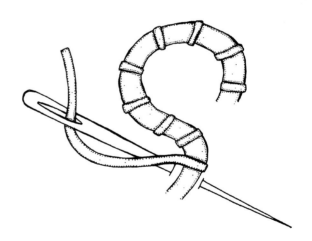

The wool or silk thread placed down to give the pattern is tacked over with sewing silk

Making Felt with Children

Children of all ages enjoy making felt. They love the warm water and soap suds, which they can play with to their hearts content, as well as the surprise element offered by the technique. If you make felt outdoors in your garden during summer, you will soon see a host of small faces pressed against  the garden fence, followed by the question: 'Can I join in?' Young children only need a piece of coloured wool for them to felt. Their lively imagination enables them to enthusiastically see a 'deer' or a 'bracelet' in their ball of wool. Small, coloured 'felt bulges' or other coincidental objects can be threaded onto a string with some beads to make a jolly necklace. It is always a delight and surprise to see how skilfully and eagerly children approach felting. Even usually naughty children are soon engrossed in their work. Although it might be expected, I have never experienced 'soap fights.' With some adult help, even six-year-olds can make recorder cases or little bags to hang around their necks. Once you have shown them how to make a ball or a picture, they can usually work independently. Children have a particularly good feeling for when the wool has been felted enough to start rubbing vigorously.

Older children enjoy felting balls to play with indoors. Get them to bring an old ball of yarn for the centre, and then they can start. Once several balls have been made, spin them all in the washing machine. This ensures they dry quickly and can be ready to play with the next day. The popular game 'knocking over tin cans' works particularly well with felt balls. Make a pyramid out of empty tin cans. The thrower stands about five metres away and tries to knock down as many cans as possible.

To play 'felt ball boules,' all players stand behind a line and try to throw or roll their ball as close as possible to an object ten to fifteen metres away.

Felt pictures (painting with fibres)

Older children love 'painting with fibres.' They are way ahead of adults when it comes to having a feel for shapes and a lack of inhibition. When given a free hand to paint their favourite things, they can create such beautiful pictures as shown below.

All these pictures were first attempts at painting with fibres. It took the children about three to four hours to make them. Before laying the wool, they sketched the picture on the cardboard background with a lead pencil. Do not use felt pens as the colour bleeds!

Sports car: Constantin, 11 years old

Cardboard background: 28 x 29 cm (11 x 11 1/2 in). Finished picture: 22 x 25 cm (8 3/4 x 10 in). Weight: 15 g (1/2 oz)

First, Constantin laid down the thin outlines with completely wet, long fibred alpaca wool. He did this with a lot of patience and skill. Next he put the windows and headlights into place, also with wet wool. Then he placed the red, *dry* wool over the whole of the car. It was only wetted with warm water once on the background, just like the blue layer, which was laid over the entire area. A layer of white wool finished off the picture. At first he had to felt very carefully, so that nothing slipped out of place. Even if it requires great patience, only turn the picture around once the felt is solid enough!

Felt ball with an elastic band

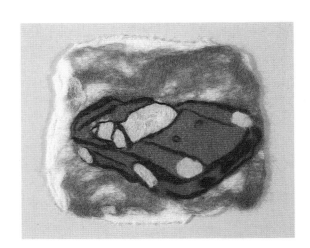

Rat: Corinne, 13 years old

Cardboard background: 29 x 26 cm (12 ¹/₂ x 10 ¹/₄ in). Finished picture: 29 x 23 cm (12 ¹/₂ x 9 in). Weight: 25 g (1 oz)

Corinne sketched her pet rat onto the cardboard. Then she placed on the eye, the left ear, the grey parts of fur and the yellow centre of the daisies. Apart from the fur, everything was wetted before being laid on the background. Then the second layer followed: pink nose, feet, tail and the white of the daisies. The white fur was again laid down over the entire body while dry, then wetted and pressed down. Then the right ear was put in place. The grass was made out of different shades of green, placed while still dry then wetted and pressed down. The blue sky was made in the same way. To finish, and to make the background, a layer of white wool was placed over the entire picture. This also gave the impression of 'fair-weather clouds.'

Clown: Wanda, 14 years old

Cardboard background: 33 x 26 cm (13 x 10 ¹/₄ in). Finished picture: 32 x 22 cm (12 ³/₄ x 8 ³/₄ in). Weight: 28 g (1 oz)

Wanda likes clowns, so she made this clown portrait. All the details that lie on the surface, like eyes, mouth, cheeks and the outline of the bow tie, were placed down first while *wet*. Then layer after layer followed, as described in the previous pictures. The clown costume worked out particularly well. After the green bow tie had been laid down and wetted, the stripes of the checked pattern came next. Only then were the squares filled in with coloured wool.

Note: Only use wet wool for outlines, small details and patterns. This lets the outlines flow, take shape and curve like the stroke of a paintbrush, as well as enabling it to stick to the cardboard background. Larger areas, on the other hand, should remain airy and can only be spread out evenly if they are dry. To ensure this, *always dry your hands before laying down the next layer of wool!*

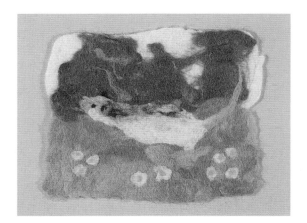

Things children enjoy felting

Younger children should not pre-sketch their pictures. Give them a little basket with coloured pieces of wool, a cardboard background, a piece of soap and a pot of warm water and let them 'draw' their favourite things.

Two rabbits, Wanda, 14 years old. The white rabbit is felted out of real Angora rabbit wool and later brushed.

Clown at night, Corinne, 13 years old

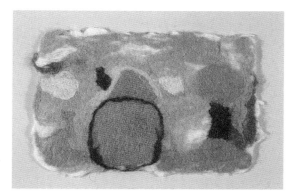

House, tree, sky: Nancy, 6 years old

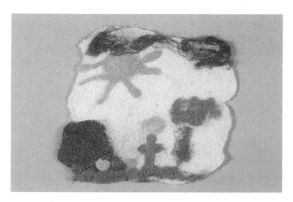

Tree, sky, sun: Julia, 6 years old

Other projects for children

- Bag embroidered with glitter
- Bag with a flap and small ball
- Bookmark
- Doll's rug

The eight-year-old felter needed some help making the small bag with a flap. See diagram for 'Felt envelope' page 67.

If you want to felt a bookmark, make sure it is not too thick as it could damage the book later.

*Bag 'embroidered with glitter,' bag with a flap
and small ball*

Bookmark

Doll's rug

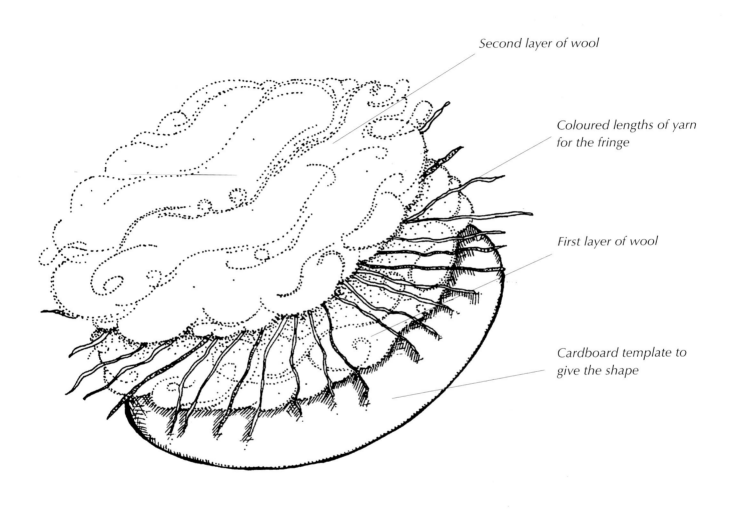

Second layer of wool

Coloured lengths of yarn for the fringe

First layer of wool

Cardboard template to give the shape

Doll's rug with a felted fringe (schematic diagram)

The Story of the Sheepdog and the Lamb

The following is a story that can inspire children to make colourful felt pictures.

Once upon a time there was a lively little lamb who was well liked by all the sheep in the flock. He had light, silky wool and a pink mouth, and his eyes were so shiny it was a pleasure to behold.

The old shaggy sheepdog also loved the little lamb and let him get away with all sorts of tricks. The little lamb enjoyed teasing the old sheepdog while she had her well-deserved rest hour. He frolicked around the dog spiritedly, poked at her from all sides and bleated loudly into her ears. Usually the old dog just blinked back in a good-natured way. But sometimes the little lamb got too bold: he ran up to the dog and rammed his forehead against her side. Then the big black animal got up, shook herself and let out a deep 'woof woof.' This was what the lamb seemed to be waiting for. He leapt away, jumping high, with the dog following close behind. Often the dog caught up with the lamb and snapped at his hind legs while growling. The mother of the lamb looked up briefly when she noticed the wild games, but continued grazing unconcerned. She had known the black dog for years and knew she was gentle and dependable. When the lamb became tired of jumping around, he went to his mother and drank her good milk. The dog went back to her work: guarding and keeping the flock together.

One day, a blue butterfly caught the little lamb's eye. He was fascinated by the way it fluttered back and forth over the flock of woolly sheep.

Inquisitively he bounded after it. He continued to follow it until, after some time, the lamb stopped and looked around, and realized that he didn't know where he was. He could not see the beautiful blue butterfly any more either, and big black clouds were gathering ominously in the sky. The solitary little lamb started bleating pitifully. Nobody answered, nobody could be seen: no sheep, no shaggy black dog, no shepherd.

Dark clouds piled up menacingly. Lightning streaked across the sky, soon followed by startling claps of thunder and not far behind, the storm and the rain. The little lost lamb strayed hither and thither, until he ended up wandering into a dark forest. He went deeper and deeper among the dense trees, and finally fell to the ground exhausted. Shivering and wet he lay in the strange, dark forest, not knowing what to do, until he was so tired he fell asleep

The shepherd and sheepdog had been very busy when the lamb had frolicked off — herding the flock into the stables before the onset of the storm. They only noticed that one lamb was missing when they heard his mother's loud, frightened bleating. The shepherd did not waste any time:

'Search, Nelly, go,' he called to the sheepdog. She knew at once what to do, and quickly found the fine, sweet smell of the lamb that she knew so well. Following her nose, she zigzagged off while the shepherd watched her leave. The thunder and lightning didn't bother her. She only stopped once to lift her head and deeply fill her lungs with air, then she ran off towards the forest and disappeared from the shepherd's view.

The little lamb was startled out of his sleep by a deep, rough bark. Then he saw a large, black shape coming towards him, and soon recognised

the sheepdog. With a feeble, drawn out 'baaa' he hurried towards the sheepdog with shaking legs. The dog panted with exertion and happiness and shook out her wet shaggy coat. Then she licked over the lamb's face with her tongue. She strongly and carefully picked up the lamb by his fur and carried him out of the woods.

Twice she had to rest, almost overcome by the effort. While carrying the lamb, she thought about the days long past when she had carried her own young in the same way. At last she reached the welcome shelter of the stables. The exhausted rescuer dropped the lamb on the hay. Both were happy to be able to rest in comfort and safety.

The lamb soon recovered and got up to find his mother. There he drank her sweet, warm milk and forgot all about his recent terrors. A few sheep had gathered around curiously to look at the lamb and the dog. Others looked from further away or bleated quietly. A peaceful atmosphere pervaded.

'Well done, my good old friend,' said the shepherd as he stroked the dog's head. She looked up at him with her clever, gentle eyes.

That evening, the shepherd decided to buy a younger dog who could learn from the wise old sheepdog and to take over the more strenuous tasks in future.

Hats

Black-brown beret

(Shaped felt)
- Cardboard template, 35 cm (14 in), allowing for shrinkage
- 90 g (3 oz) wool

This classic beret has one special feature: it is made out of two thirds sheep's wool and one third dog wool. Both wools are almost exactly the same colour and were mixed together with hand carders.

Place the wool in even layers around the template. Wet each layer. Only once the felting test is successful, cut out the inner circle narrowly. The opening will still widen with wear!

Violet beret

(Shaped felt)
- Cardboard template, 35 cm (14 in), allowing for shrinkage
- 80 g (3 oz) wool

This hat is made out of half sheep's wool (night blue) and half Angora rabbit wool (dyed with cochineal). The wools were *not* carded together.

First spread out the Angora wool around the cardboard template. You will need skill and patience to do this, as the wool 'flies away' and sticks to your hands. Using a lot of water, you can make the Angora wool stick to the template. Then spread out the sheep's wool over the Angora wool. Press down well, soap and felt. Turn the hat inside out so the sheep's wool is on the inside, and the fluffy Angora wool on the outside. Brush it well once it has dried. Because this piece has a large amount of Angora wool, it will take longer to felt than the black-brown beret.

12.1   *Black-brown beret*

12.2   *Violet beret*

Note: If the beret does not fit well because the opening has been cut too large, sew a ribbon around its edge. Alternatively, you can embroider a row of chain stitches around the edge, and then crochet a few rows of single crochet stitches.

Boy's hat with feather

Hiking hat with sheep

Boy's hat with a feather

(Shaped felt)
- Cardboard template (see figure 12.5)
- 80 g (3 oz) wool

Divide the wool into four equal parts for the layers. Spread the first layer out vertically over the template, wet it and pull the wool a few centimetres over the edges of the template. Turn the template around, and spread out the second layer in the same way. Then spread out the third layer horizontally, wet it and pull it a few centimetres over the edges of the template. Turn the template around again and place the last layer horizontally. Once everything has been distributed, wetted and pulled into shape, check for thin areas. The tip of the hat may need special attention; if necessary add some extra wool. The brim can be slightly thinner. Only cut open the hat at the brim after successfully testing the felt. Remove the template, turn the hat inside out and lay it down flat with the edges in the centre. If you have pressed the sides well against the template, there will not be any bulges in this area, but if there are, vigorous felting, massaging and fulling can still even them out.

Finish shaping the hat directly on the child's head. To do this, put a bathing cap on the child's head, and place the warm, well-soaped hat on top. Rub, press and massage with both hands. Keep rotating the hat around the head and turn it inside out every now and again. Rub and shape the brim between the palms of your hand until it has the desired form. In between, stand the hat onto the fulling board to full and smooth the brim. Then soap the hat up again, put it back on and continue felting until it fits.

You should allow at least one to two hours for felting a hat.

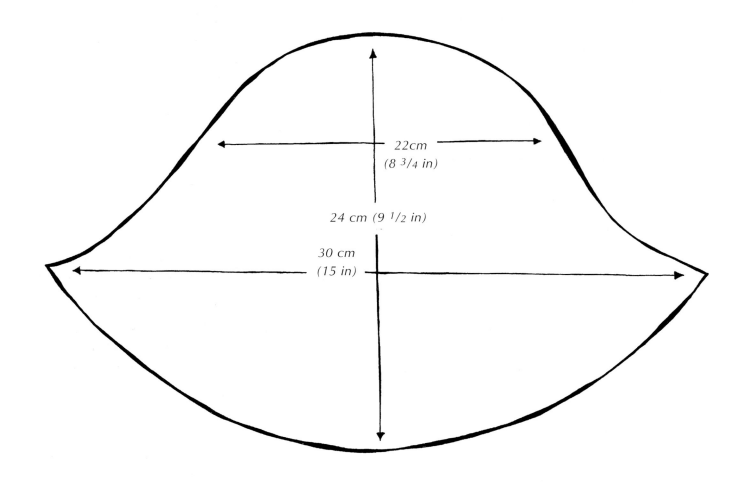

22cm
(8 ³/4 in)

24 cm (9 ¹/2 in)

30 cm
(15 in)

The grey hiking hat with appliquéd sheep was made following this same template, slightly enlarged

12.5 *Template for 'Boy's hat with feather' for a head circumference of approx. 53 cm (21 in)*

Purple hat with grape decoration

(Shaped felt)

- Cardboard template (see figure 12.7)
- 100–120 g (3 $^1/_2$–4 oz) wool (half white, half violet)
- About 30 g (1 oz) green wool for the grapes
- A piece of white sample felt for the leaf

First, wind the violet wool around the template, then the white wool, which will later be the inside of the hat. Felt and full as described for the boy's hat.

Note: This hat has a high crown. Only press it down and shape after rinsing. To dry, stand the hat on a towel on its brim, smooth well and press everything into shape.

12.6   *Purple hat with grape decoration*

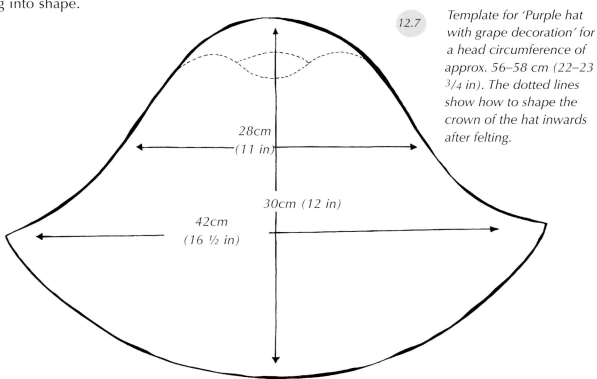

28cm
(11 in)

30cm (12 in)

42cm
(16 ½ in)

12.7   *Template for 'Purple hat with grape decoration' for a head circumference of approx. 56–58 cm (22–23 ³/4 in). The dotted lines show how to shape the crown of the hat inwards after felting.*

Jewellery

Oak leaf pin brooch

Cut the green leaf, length about 10 cm (4 in), out of a very thick, solid piece of sample felt. Using tight backstitch, embroider veins on the leaf.

Each acorn requires about 2 g of wool. First wind a very firm ball and felt it (see 'Felting small balls' page 34). Once the ball is stable, roll it vigorously into the acorn shape between the palms of your hands. To make the acorn cups, wind some wool around a small template which is slightly larger than the finished acorn, and felt it. Once it is solid enough, cut it in half. This makes two acorn cups. Continue felting them individually by turning them over the tip of your forefinger. To fasten the acorn and cup together take a needle and insert it through the leaf, then up through the cup, straight through the middle of the acorn. Pick up a bead and then push the needle back down the same way.

13.1   *Oak leaf pin brooch*

Cherry pin brooch

Cut the leaves out of a piece of thick, solid sample felt and round off the edges. Sew the leaf veins with tight backstitches. For each cherry, wind 2 g of red wool into a firm ball and felt.

13.2   *Cherry pin brooch*

Grape pin brooch

Felt thirteen little balls of about 2 g each (use letter scales) and sew them into a bunch of grapes. Cut the leaf out of a not too thin piece of sample felt. Sew the leaf veins very tightly.

The oak, cherry and grape decorations are fixed to a pin brooch. Depending on your preference, these pin brooches can be fastened to a hat (see figure 13.6), coat or shoes.

Orange necklace

Felt nine small, very firm balls, 2.5 g each. Once they have dried, thread them onto an orange leather string alternating them with seeds and wooden beads (see figure 13.3).

13.3   *Orange necklace and necklace with shell*

Necklace with shell

The shell depicted is from the beach in Copacabana. The hole was there already; drilled by a shell-eating marine animal. Two solid felt balls, matching the colours of the shell, and a matching leather string make the shell the centre-piece of an attractive necklace (see figure 13.3).

Felt setting for a semi-precious stone

First cut out a template the shape of the stone, allowing 1.5 cm (3/4 in) extra around it for shrinkage. Wind around the template with wool in a colour that suits the stone, and felt. After testing the felt, cut open and remove the template. Place the stone in it and continue felting around it.

The felt cover should encase the stone tightly, so do not make the opening too wide. To hang it around your neck, fasten a leather string to the inside.

This is a nice gift, particularly for boys and men (see figure 13.4).

13.4   *Felt setting for large semi-precious stone, hair slide (barrette), violet necklace*

Hair slide (barrette)

Thread four very firm, different coloured small felt balls (each 2 g, letter scales!) and three ceramic discs onto a thin nylon thread (fishing line). Fasten them firmly onto a hair slide.

This unusual hair slide goes well with the following necklace (see figure 13.4).

Violet necklace

Felt 21 little balls (2 g each) and thread them alternately with ceramic discs onto a leather string, using a long, pointed needle (see figure 13.4).

Friendship rings

(Layered balls, modelled felt)
One ball will make two rings. You will need some felting experience for this project.
- Five different colours of wool
- Key ring or a very large, simple cheap ring
- Needle and thread
- Very sharp knife or a scalpel – careful, keep it away from children!

Wind a small ball using the centre colour and felt lightly.

Evenly wind the second colour around it, lightly felt. Continue in the same way until you have used all five colours. This soft ball should be approximately 3 cm (1 1/4 in) diameter. Once finished it will reduce to 2.5 cm (1 in) diameter.

For further instructions, see 'Melon' page 104.

13.5   *Friendship rings*

Note: Do not spin this finished ball in the washing machine, as instructed for the melon.

The next step is great fun. Place a wooden board underneath the ball and cut it in half with a sharp knife or scalpel. This will reveal the colours and show whether you felted long and energetically enough! All the layers should be well connected, the coloured bands clearly and evenly set apart from each other.

Wind wool, in the colour matching the last layer of the ball, closely around the ring. Felt between your hands and on your finger.

Fasten the half-ball carefully and very securely to the ring (with a needle and thread).

Cover the seam with small bits of wool, adding more wool to the ring until it fits your finger.

Wind a very thin layer of wool several times crosswise over the connecting point between ring and half-ball. Felt each layer.

While felting, repeatedly slip the ring on your finger and twist to felt the inside. Vigorously rub the connecting points repeatedly over the palm of your hand. Continue to stroke and massage until you are pleased with the result. The whole ring should feel firm, the half-ball neither wobbly nor loose.

Make the second ring in the same way. You could choose a different ring colour to make them slightly different.

To finish, knot the rings into a sock and add to the next 60°C (140°F) washing machine cycle to make them even firmer.

Heart and flower necklaces

(Shaped felt, felt cords, felt ball, flat felt)
- Approximately 10 g (1/3 oz) wool for an entire necklace
- Cardboard
- Needle with a very large eye

Make a small piece of flat felt between the palms of your hands. Cut out a flower centre or heart shape. Cut a flower or heart-shaped template out of cardboard (see figures 13.7 and 13.8). Wet the small felt shape and 'stick' it to the template.

Then layer the wool around the template, wet through, soap and felt.

Mark the back of the flower or heart pendant with different coloured wool to avoid inadvertently cutting into the wrong side. See 'Heart bags' page 139.

Cut a small horizontal slit into the back, remove the cardboard, turn right side out, push your finger inside and shape.

Make two felt cords, about 50 cm (19 3/4 in) long (see page 36).

There are several ways you can attach the cords to the pendant: You can pull the cords through the back, leaving the pendant open at the back so the owner can keep a lucky charm or small letter in it. Alternatively, felt the cords to the back of the pendant (figure 13.9). Sew the slit shut with a few stitches, sew the cords to the back, place some wool over the seam, wet, add soap and carefully felt the cords in place.

Necklace fastener
Bend the felt cord back to make a loop at one end of the necklace. Tie it firmly in place with a strand of wool and felt. Make a small felt ball (see page 34), just large enough to fit through the loop. Using the needle, string the cords through the ball and knot the ends.

13.6   *Heart and flower necklaces*

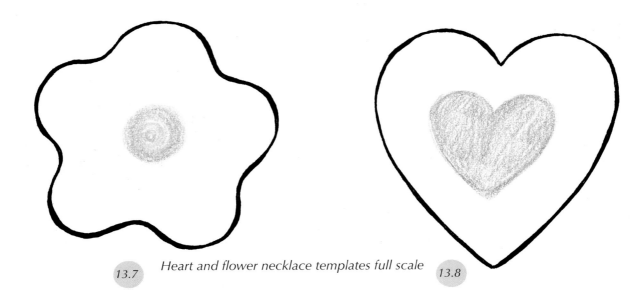

13.7   *Heart and flower necklace templates full scale*   13.8

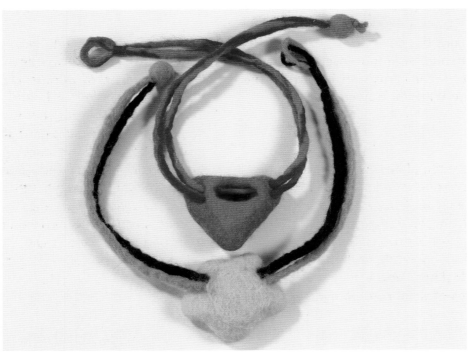

13.9   *Two ways to attach the strings to the pendant:*
1. Pull it through (heart); 2. Place on and felt over (flower)

For Cold Feet

Hot water bottle cover

- Cardboard template: the outline of your hot water bottle + 3 cm (1 1/4 in)
- 120 g (4 oz) wool (here half red, half natural brown)
- A few tufts of coloured wool for the pattern

Lay a pattern onto the template with the coloured wool (see 'Painting with fibres' page 41). Spread the red wool over it in layers, then the brown wool, and then felt and full lightly. Cut the cover about 14 cm (5 1/2 in) inwards at the top, remove the cardboard, turn the cover inside out and felt and full the patterned side too. Insert the *empty* hot water bottle. It can remain in its cover even when being filled with hot water.

Insoles

- Cardboard template: outline of the foot (remember one template for the right foot, one for the left foot!) + 2–3 cm (3/4–1 1/4 in) for shrinkage.
- 30–50 g (1–1 3/4 oz) wool for both soles, depending on the size and desired thickness. You can also use leftover pieces of wool carded together to make the insoles.

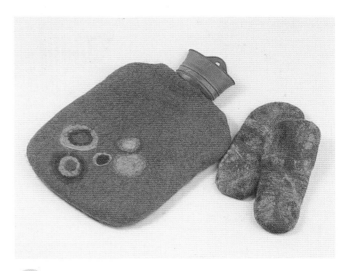

14.1   Hot water bottle cover, insoles

Wind the wool evenly around the cardboard insoles. Be careful at the heel and toe, as this is where the layers of wool tend to slip.

For particularly thick and firm insoles (for example, an insole for rubber Wellington boots), do not remove the cardboard after felting! Iron the insoles after they have dried. Otherwise, make a small slit at the heel and remove the cardboard. Sew the seam shut and felt this area again.

You can make two thin insoles by winding around one template, and then cutting the finished sole apart around the edges.

Full all insoles well, as otherwise they wear out quickly!

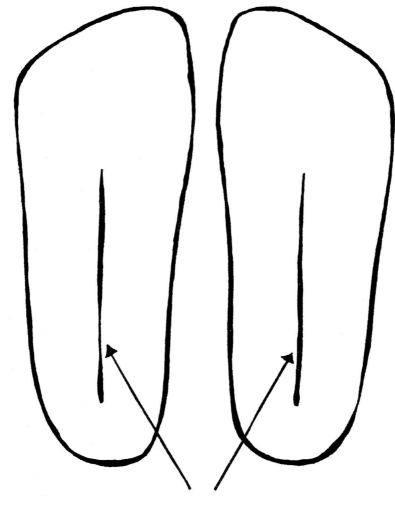

Slits approximately
14 cm (5 $^1/_2$ in) long

14.2 Mushroom slippers. Cut a slit approx. 14 cm (5 $^1/_2$ in) along the upper side of each raw finished sole.

Mushroom slippers

Once you have successfully felted a pair of insoles you will also be able to make these beautiful slippers.

- Two cardboard templates (see 'Insoles', figure 14.1 and figure 14.2).
- A European shoe size 38 (UK size 5, USA size 7) requires 40–50 g (1 $\frac{1}{2}$– 1 $\frac{3}{4}$ oz) wool *per shoe;* half white, half coloured, allowing some white wool for the spots.

Place the white dots onto the later *upper side* only. For dotted patterns see page 35.

Wind the red wool in thin, spread out layers around the template, wetting every layer with hot water and pressing down. Repeat with the white wool.

Do *not* forget which shoe you are working on and mistakenly cut the sole open.

Note: Make the sole, heel and toe slightly thicker. Felt and full vigorously. Cut a slit about 14 cm (5 $\frac{1}{2}$ in) vertically along the top of the shoe (see template figure 14.2). Remove the cardboard. Rinse out the shoe thoroughly and put it to one side. Repeat the process for the second shoe. Then turn both shoes inside out.

If the cuts seem too short at first, do not lengthen them right away. Usually they stretch by themselves when putting the slippers on and taking them off. At this stage, the slippers are usually far too big and hang formlessly on your feet. This will soon change!

Now, using both hands, alternate between rubbing and massaging the slippers vigorously against your feet, kneading the heels and toes. You can rest your foot on the edge of the

14.3   *Mushroom slippers*

bathtub or a chair. Put a mat on the floor to prevent slipping while wearing the soapy shoes. In between, sit down on a chair with the felting board or washboard at your feet and rub your feet back and forth on it, as if cleaning your shoes on a doormat. Let the inner sides of the shoes rub against each other too. With one foot rub repeatedly against the upper part of the other slipper. Use plenty of warm water and soap

This task is quite arduous. It is easier if you have a helper. The reward for your efforts is a pair of wonderful, perfectly fitting, home made slippers!

Note: The slippers will soon wear through if they do not have a leather sole. Cut the soles out of soft leather and glue them onto the felt sole with shoemaker's glue. Then briefly press the shoes between two boards with a vice.

Woollen boots

(Shaped felt)
You will get two boots from one template. Use a pair of shoes that fit to make the template. Both boots are made with one template attached at the top of the bootleg (see diagram figure 14.5). This makes them more even, and also saves time as you can felt them both simultaneously. Make sure the cardboard is not too thin!

- European shoe size 38 (UK size 5, USA size 7) and a bootleg of approximately 8 cm (3 1/4 in) requires 170 g (6 oz) wool (half white, half coloured) *per shoe.* Use long staple wool!

If desired, first wind a few coloured strands of wool around the template as a decoration. Then place the coloured wool layer for layer, alternating it horizontally and vertically around the template. Repeat this process with the white wool.

Note: Wind an extra layer around the toes, heels and soles. To give the whole thing more stability, wind woollen yarn around the whole wet wool package. This little 'trick' also makes it a lot easier to keep the shape while felting. Felting a pair of boots takes a few hours and is not recommended for beginners. It is helpful if two people share the work.

After successfully testing the felt, cut the raw boots apart at the bootleg, then turn them inside out and work on the coloured side. Cut a slit about 8 cm (3¼ in) down the front of the bootleg. Gently squeeze the boots out in warm water, soap them and put them on. Then continue in the same way as for the 'mushroom slippers.' This is where

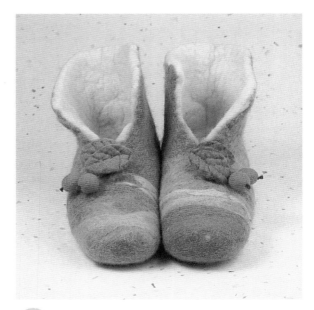

14.4   Woollen boots

help is useful. The helper can kneel in front of the 'boot owner,' and work vigorously on the boots and feet therein. Take the boots off at intervals and full them as forcefully as possible on the felting board. Then continue felting the boots on your feet until they fit well.

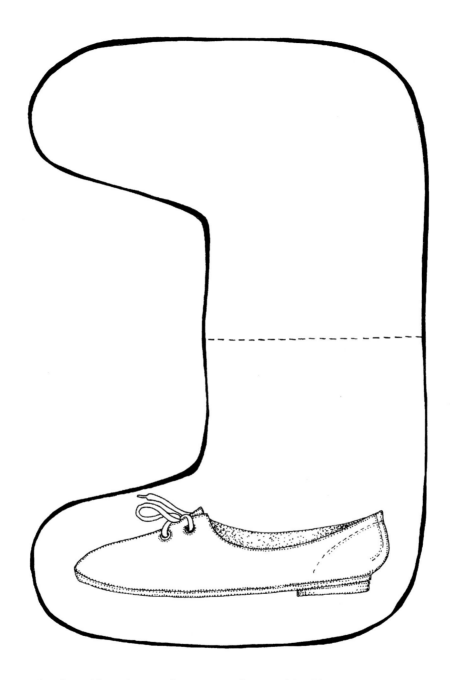

Woollen boots. The dotted line shows where to cut the raw felted boots apart. To make the template use a shoe that fits to obtain the correct size.

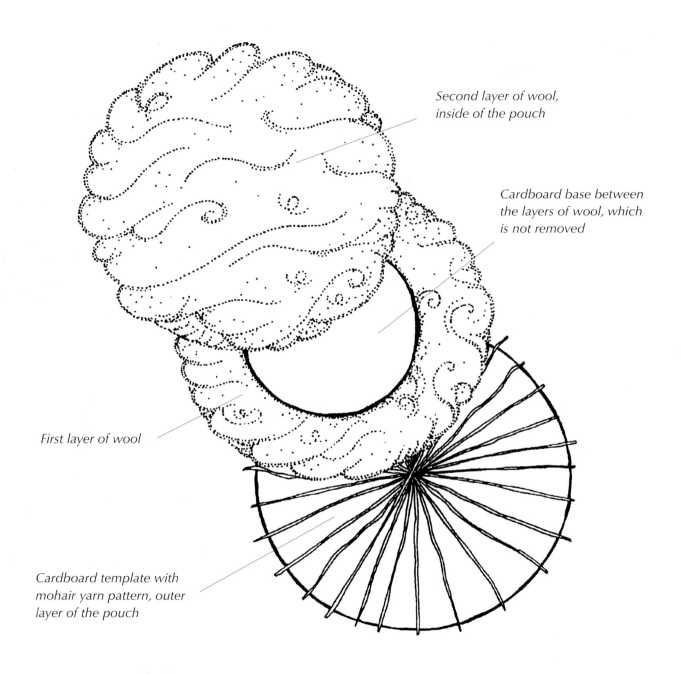

Second layer of wool,
inside of the pouch

Cardboard base between
the layers of wool, which
is not removed

First layer of wool

Cardboard template with
mohair yarn pattern, outer
layer of the pouch

15.1   Gift pouch (schematic diagram)

Beautiful Gift-wrap

These gift-wraps have the advantage that they can be re-used, or used for other things later. They are also very individual and original.

Pouches

(Flat felt piece)

Large pouch
- Cardboard circle, 29 cm (11 $^1/_2$ in)
- Base circle, 11 cm (4 $^1/_2$ in)
- 50 g (1 $^3/_4$ oz) wool (half red, half purple)
- Mohair yarn, dark purple

Small pouch
- Cardboard circle, 24 cm (9 $^1/_2$ in)
- Base circle, 9 cm (3 $^1/_2$ in)
- 30 g (1 oz) wool, natural white
- Mohair yarn, pink

These simple pouches can be made in any size. Their special feature is the cardboard base between the felt layers, which is not removed. This gives the pouch a better shape as well as a base to stand on. Do not make the base out of corrugated cardboard; the back of a sketch block is better suited.

Make the striped pattern by laying coloured strands of mohair yarn in a radial pattern onto the cardboard circle before layering the wool. During felting the yarn felts to the wool layers above (see diagram figure 15.1).

How to make the pouch
1. Place the yarn onto the template.
2. Lay the first layer of wool on top, wet it and press it down.
3. Place the cardboard base in the centre.
4. Lay the second layer of wool on top. Wet it, press it down and felt.

Note: Make sure the felt has a nice rounded shape. Use the edge of your hand to rub around the edges repeatedly, and rub inwards more often than outwards!

Once the finished bag has dried, iron it to straighten out the cardboard base between the wool layers. To finish, thread a string or a leather thong around the edge. Bags with a different coloured inside are also pretty.

15.2 *Party bag with red dots and satin ribbon, two round gift pouches*

Party bag with red dots and satin ribbon

(Shaped felt)
- Cardboard template (see figure 15.3), allowing for shrinkage
- 40 g (1 ½ oz) white wool
- Some red wool for the dots

First arrange the dots on the template (see 'Painting with fibres' page 35). Then spread out the white wool in layers on top and felt. Only cut the top open after testing that the felt is finished.

Note: Wind the satin ribbon very tightly around the bag while it is still damp. This creates nice folds at the top of the bag.

The bag can be used to hide all sorts of surprises.

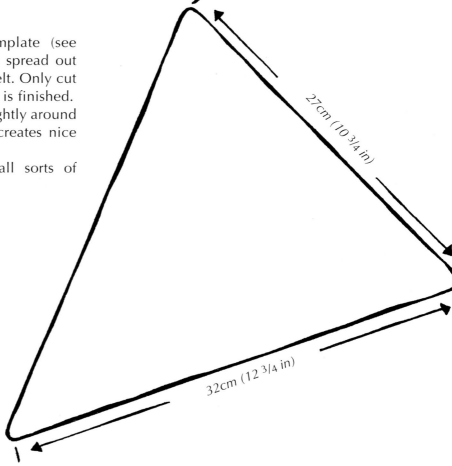

27cm (10 3/4 in)

32cm (12 3/4 in)

15.3   *Template for 'Party bag with red dots'*

Large felt bag with colourful stars

(Shaped felt)

- Cardboard template (see figure 15.5), allowing for shrinkage
- 80 g (2 ³/4 oz) wool (half orange, half white)
- Some coloured tufts of wool

First lay the stars on the template with long staple, coloured wool. To do this, completely wet very thin strands of wool, so they adhere to the template (see 'Painting with fibres' page 35). Spread out the first layer of orange wool around the template and wet it with hot water. Then wind the white wool around the template. Later this will be the inside.

Note: Make sure the wool does not slip at the point of the bag. Only cut the bag open at the upper diagonal edge after testing the felt. Then turn it inside out and continue felting.

Your gift will keep particularly well in this beautiful bag.

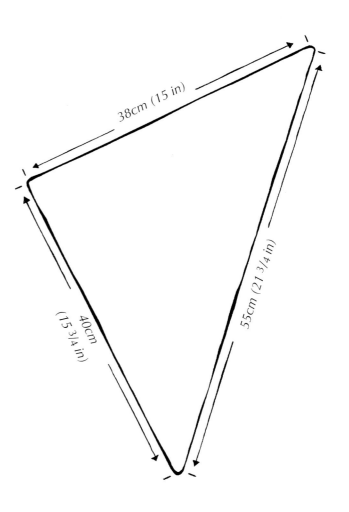

15.4   *Large felt bag with colourful stars*

15.5   *Template for 'Large felt bag with colourful stars'*

Large envelope

(Combination of shaped felt and flat felt)

- Cardboard template (see figure 15.7), allowing for shrinkage
- 120 g (4 1/4 oz) wool, natural white
- Some red wool for the 'seal'
- A large press-stud

Wind the wool in layers around the rectangular envelope enclosure, that is, the 'bag'. This is the shaped felt. By contrast, only place a flat layer of wool on the triangular flap.

Once the felt is firm enough, remove the cardboard template, turn inside out and continue felting. To finish, full briefly. Felt the red wool into a round seal between your palms to cover the press-stud later.

This large envelope is a beautiful gift-wrap for writing paper or any writing implements. It can later be used for keeping letters in.

Note: This envelope is the basic shape for all bags with a flap, and can be varied to suit your taste.

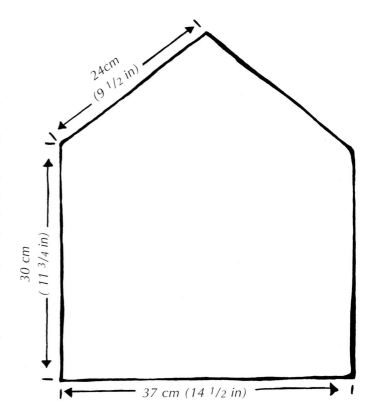

24cm (9 1/2 in)

30 cm (11 3/4 in)

37 cm (14 1/2 in)

15.6　*Felt envelope*

15.7　*Measurements for template of 'Large envelope'*

Only lay wool on one side of the flap (flat felt)

BACK

Wind the wool around the template for the enclosure

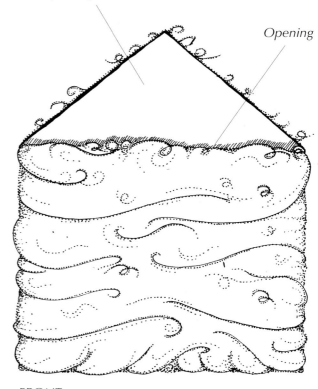

Do not put any wool here!

Opening

FRONT

15.8   *How to wind wool around the template to make the felt envelope*

Felted Things for a Baby

Rattle ball

To make the 'inner life' hollow out a cork and insert a small bell into it, or fill a small tin or plastic container with bells, rice, stones or beads, depending on whether you want the ball to rustle, tinkle or rattle.

Firmly wind strands of wool or cloth around this centre, until the whole ball is evenly round and has nearly reached the desired size. Then spread a white layer of wool over the ball and wet it thoroughly. Finally, wind the coloured, well-teased wool around the ball in several thin layers. Dip your hands into warm water and lather them up. First, gently roll, form and press the ball between your hands. The more the wool felts, the more vigorously you can knead it. Towards the end, felt the ball with full strength, like making a hard snowball, using plenty of hot water and soap. Rinse under running cold water and squeeze it out firmly. Spin it in the washing machine.

Note: You can make attractive patterns by winding coloured threads around the ball before felting.

Use an old ball of wool as the inside to make a ball without a rattle.

Variation: This toy can be made more interesting for older children by fastening a thin, strong elastic band to the ball (see page 41).

Teething ring

Wind long staple, coloured wool — if possible plant-dyed — around a wooden ring. Immerse the firmly wound ring in hot water and lather up your hands well. Grasp the ring with both hands while turning it.

Note: A colourful, suitably sized ring can also be used as bracelet.

16.1   *Rattle ball and teething ring*

Bottle warmer

(Shaped felt)
- For a 250 ml ($^1/_4$ quart) bottle:
- Cardboard template, 19.5 x 9 cm (7 $^3/_4$ x 3 $^3/_4$ in), allowing for shrinkage
- 30 g (1 oz) wool (half white, half coloured)
- Some mohair yarn

First, wind the mohair yarn around the template. Then place an extra layer of wool — in this case pink — around the base to make it more durable. Wind the remaining wool in layers around the template, wetting and pressing down each layer. Then felt.

After 15 to 20 minutes, once the unfinished item is fairly stable, cut open the top and remove the damp cardboard. Turn the whole thing inside out and also felt the coloured side well. Then full.

Push the bottle into the case and continue felting, working the base particularly well to ensure that the bottle will stand securely later. Roll the felt cover (with the bottle inside) back and forth along the felting board, then, with the bottle standing upright, vigorously full the base on the felting board. Take the cover off again and rinse out the soap thoroughly. To dry, put the bottle back in the bottle warmer. It should fit tightly. Wind a cord around the top.

This felt cover is washable and any milk, juice or tea stains can be easily removed!

16.2   *Bottle cover*

69

Covers to Protect and Decorate

Recorder cases

- Cardboard template: outline of the recorder + 2 cm (3/4 in) to allow for shrinkage
- Approximately 60 g (2 oz) wool (half natural white, half coloured) is required for a soprano recorder

First, wind a layer of wool around both ends of the template, as the recorder needs most protection here. Wind the rest of the wool in several thin layers evenly around the template like a bandage, wetting each layer with warm water and pressing it down. Wind right up to the ends, adding an extra layer of wool there now and again. It is important there are no holes or thin areas there.

Note: Recorder cases cannot be turned inside out later. They are too narrow and the opening too small. For this reason, lay down the white layer of wool first, and felt from the coloured or patterned outer layer. Recorder cases need to be felted particularly energetically for a satisfactory result.

After successfully testing the felt, cut a small slit about 5 cm (2 in) below the upper end. This prevents the recorder from slipping out later.

Pull out the damp cardboard and re-felt the cut. Then vigorously full the whole piece.

Later, attach a string so you can hang the recorder around your neck.

The three recorder cases pictured have different patterns:
1. After spreading out the orange layers of wool, coloured yarns were wound around the template.
2. White recorder case with coloured 'marbled' effect.
3. Red recorder case decorated with a few strands of coloured wool.

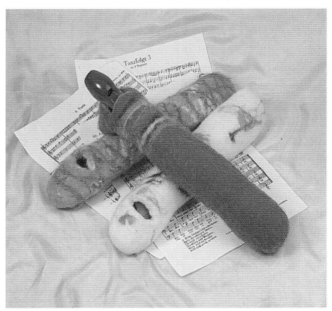

17.1   *Recorder cases*

Glasses cases

Red-brown glasses case
- Cardboard template: outline of the spectacles + 2 cm ($^3/_4$ in) to allow for shrinkage
- 20 g ($^3/_4$ oz) wool, natural brown
- 20 g ($^3/_4$ oz) wool, madder red

First, spread the brown wool (or your preferred outer colour) around the template, then lay the red wool on top. Felt! Cut the horizontal opening about 3–4 cm (1 $^1/_4$–1 $^3/_4$in) below the upper curve.

White Angora case for children's glasses
- Cardboard template: see above
- 20 g ($^3/_4$ oz) wool, natural white
- 20 g ($^3/_4$ oz) Angora rabbit wool

First, spread out the Angora rabbit wool, then place the sheep's wool on top. It is much easier to felt the sheep's wool first, as the fine Angora wool slips around to start with. Once the sheep's wool has connected well to the Angora wool — after about 20 minutes of intense felting — cut the piece open lengthwise and turn it inside out. Now the Angora side can be felted without a problem. After the case has dried, brush it with a soft hairbrush until fluffy. This glasses case is decorated with scattered, pink, sweet-water pearls.

Red glasses case with embroidery
- Cardboard template: as described above
- 30 g (1 oz) wool, madder/cochineal red
- 10 g ($^1/_3$ oz) Tussah silk wool

Lay the silk thinly and evenly around the template, then spread out the wool on top. After about 30 minutes of felting, cut the piece open at the upper edge, remove the cardboard, turn inside out and continue felting.

In this case, the silk is the lining. As silk hardly felts, it can only be used for extremely thin layers, the wool fibres still have to 'reach through.'

The red case is decorated with a simple floral pattern embroidered with silk threads and glass beads.

17.2   *Glasses cases*

Book covers

Here are two suggestions for hand felting book covers:
1. Flat book cover (for beginners)
2. Book cover with shaped sleeve pockets (for advanced felters)

- Approximately 60–70 g (2–2 1/2 oz) wool is required for a book of 23 x15 cm (9 x 6 in) and 4 cm (1 1/3 in) thick.

1. Flat book cover

Cut out a cardboard rectangle the size of the book, adding 5–7 cm (2–2 3/4 in) at each end for folding back the sleeve pocket, and allowing 2 cm (3/4 in) all around for shrinkage. Spread out the wool, alternating vertical and horizontal layers, *onto* the cardboard template and felt.

It is particularly important to make a neat rectangular form for a book cover. Use the edge of your hand to repeatedly stroke around the outlines of the form and rub inwards more often than outwards.

Once the felt is fairly stable after about 20–30 minutes, turn the piece over and felt the back. Once the felt is dry (you can also iron it), place it around the book, fold the sides back and sew them in place. Felt along the seams again to make them less obvious.

2. Book cover with shaped sleeve pocket

Remember when cutting out the cardboard template that you do *not* need the 5–7 cm (2–2 3/4 in) for folding back the sides. Instead, wind the wool layers *around* the template at the side for a couple of centimetres. This means the sleeve pockets that hold the book cover in place

17.3   Book covers

are felted from the start, not sewn later as in the above suggestion.

Note: Pay particular attention to the corners. They should not be too thin or threadbare. The felted shaped pockets must be firmly felted to the front of the cover.

Tips for making the checked pattern

Wind one long length of yarn around the cardboard template, once vertically, once horizontally. Then place the layers of wool on the template. Once the cover has been felted, cut away the threads on the inside of the template where there are no wool layers.

About the photos (figure 17.3)

1. Violet book cover, marbled, with appliquéd star and rod beads: The shooting star decorating this book cover already suggests the book's content — a collection of Christmas stories.
2. Red checked book cover: The checked pattern is neutral and suits many books. See 'Creative Possibilities' page 34.

Treasure bags

(Two bags for each template, see 'Basic Instructions' page 24)

Treasure or 'lucky' bags are always useful, so make two at a time. This is not much more work than felting one, and you will have an additional beautiful gift.

- Cardboard template: see template figure 17.6
- 40–50 g (1 $\frac{1}{2}$ –1 $\frac{3}{4}$ oz) wool, depending on size (half white, half coloured)

The template's basic shape is oval, but it can be varied to suit your taste; an hourglass shape will later give a narrow opening, a wider centre allows you to make folds at the sides etc. You can then decorate these treasure bags with patterns (see 'Creative Possibilities' page 34).

After felting and successfully testing the felt, cut the whole packet exactly in half. Remove the cardboard, turn the bags inside out and continue felting them separately. Make sure you massage away any bulges which might have developed at the edges of the template. Felt the bag by turning it over your fist every now and again. To finish, full it gently.

The treasure bags shown here are decorated with felt balls and leaves, or with embroidered silk threads and glass beads (Indian beads, figure 17.4). All of them were lined with cloth, some with silk, and have a cord to hang them up by. The small felt balls also serve as buttons. The black-brown bag (figure 17.5) is made out of 100% dog hair, mainly the under wool (winter fur!). The sides were folded inwards while still damp, and then the bag was dried flat between two towels and weighted down. This ensures the folds stay permanently.

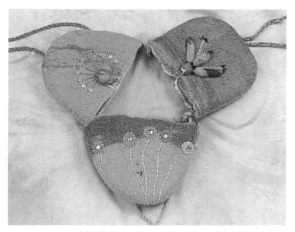

17.4   *Treasure bags*

17.5   *Treasure bags*

73

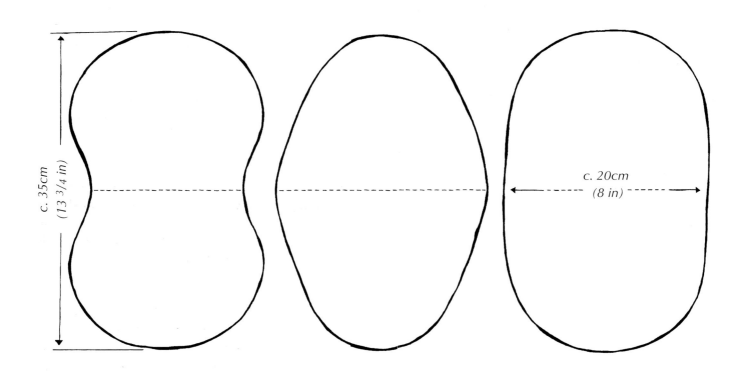

c. 35cm
(13 ¾ in)

c. 20cm
(8 in)

17.6   *Templates for 'treasure bags,' two per template. The dotted lines show where to cut apart the raw felt bags*

Dolls

Dolls have been incredibly popular toys throughout history. Among every child's play things, dolls have a special place and are equally important to boys and girls. They are the image of the human in the soul of the child. For this reason they should be chosen with great care.

It is nice if the first doll is handmade; if possible by a person who is close to the child. Do not scrimp on time or effort whilst making the doll. Only use high quality, natural materials to suit the receptive senses of the child. The doll should be made as simply as possible to give the child space for their developing imagination.

As the following examples show, it is possible to hand felt a complete doll. These dolls are extremely durable.

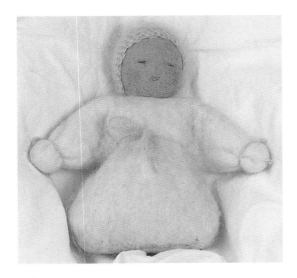

18.1   Sack doll

Sack doll

(Body: shaped felt; head: felt ball, circumference approximately 19 cm (7 1/2 in))

- Cardboard template (see figure 18.2), allowing for shrinkage
- 50 g (1 3/4 oz) wool for the body, in this case a hand-carded mixture of 30 g (1 oz) Friesian sheep wool, 10 g (1/3 oz) Angora rabbit wool, 10 g (1/3 oz) mohair goat wool
- 50 g (1 3/4 in) wool for the head: inner core, leftover wool yarn, approximately 25 g (1 oz); outer layer, skin coloured wool, approximately 25 g (1 oz)
- Some wool to stuff

You should have some felting experience before attempting to hand felt an entire doll. You should allow two to three days to make this doll! Well-made hand-felted dolls are nearly indestructible and keep their shape extremely well.

Head

It is easier to make the body fit the size of the head than vice versa. To start with, make the head like a ball: wind a very solid ball out of leftover yarn. Wind the skin coloured wool over the surface in several thin layers and press down each layer with wet, soaped hands. Carefully form it into a nice round ball. Then start vigorously rolling the ball in one direction between your palms until a firm oval shape develops. If your hands get tired, ask someone else to take over. Do not stop felting too early; *the head has to be very solid!* To finish, thoroughly rinse under running water (knead and squeeze it).

A simple trick to give the head a good shape: bind off the head tightly with a very stable, thick length of thread.

Note: remember the small child model — high forehead, small chin — make sure you do not bind off too high. Put a small piece of cardboard between the back of the head and the thread, as there is no need for an indentation here, and this is where the knot is. Use a thread that will not bleed, as traces of colour on the damp head will spoil it. The bound off head can be spun in a washing machine. Only remove the thread once the head is completely dry and has been sewn onto the body.

Body

The body is made out of a thick piece of shaped felt (see figure 18.2). Place an extra layer of wool over the neck area (where the head is later attached), as it needs to be particularly stable. The relatively heavy head will wobble on too thin shoulders. Cut a slit at most 8 cm (3 1/4 in) long at the base of the sack (the only opening) to remove the cardboard, and then stuff the body.

Spin the felted and rinsed body in the washing machine. Stuff the arms with some wool while the body is still damp. Do not stuff the top of the arms, otherwise they will stick out stiffly from the body. Bind off the hands with a thin thread. Arrange the arms in a natural position and leave them to dry.

Attaching the head

First, place a very thick piece of trial felt on the inside between the shoulders where the head will be sewn on later. Take a very long needle and push it through this piece of sample felt, to come out between the shoulders at the place where the head will be attached. Then push it lengthwise up through the head to its crown. Push the needle back down again a few millimetres, beside the point where the needle emerged. Repeat the entire process again. This makes a small cross at the crown of the head. Pull the thread tightly and sew it in on the piece of trial felt in the chest.

This attaches the head to the body in a basic way, but it is still fairly wobbly. Sew the head to the body from the outside with skin coloured thread, stitching around the head three or four times with small, almost invisible, stitches. Make sure the head does not wobble!

To finish, stuff the chest and stomach with some wool. The body should remain soft and pliable. Do not stuff too tightly!

Sew the cut at the base of the body shut with small stitches. Wet this seam, soap it and felt over it again. Brush the body lightly.

Wind a thin cord around the chest. Hint at eyes and mouth with a few stitches. If desired, lightly redden the checks with a coloured pencil. A crocheted hat protects the head.

The pink glow of the body comes from the red layer of wool beneath the white layers (colour combinations!).

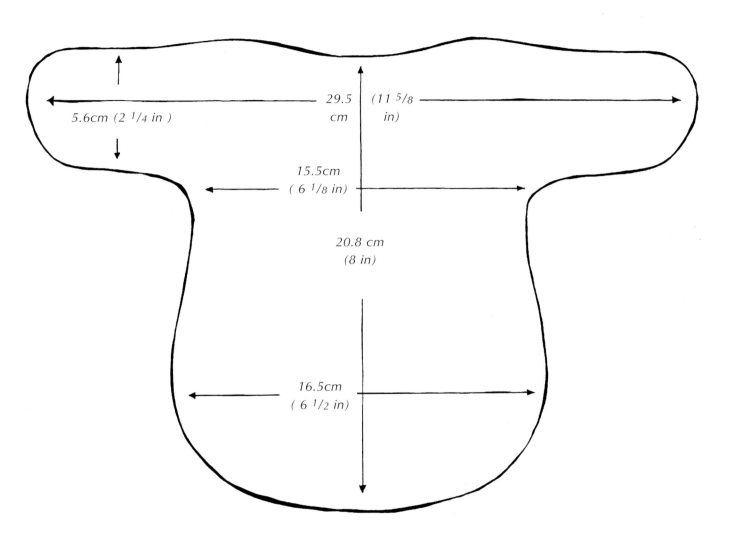

5.6cm (2 1/4 in)

29.5 cm

(11 5/8 in)

15.5cm (6 1/8 in)

20.8 cm (8 in)

16.5cm (6 1/2 in)

18.2   *Template for 'Sack doll'*

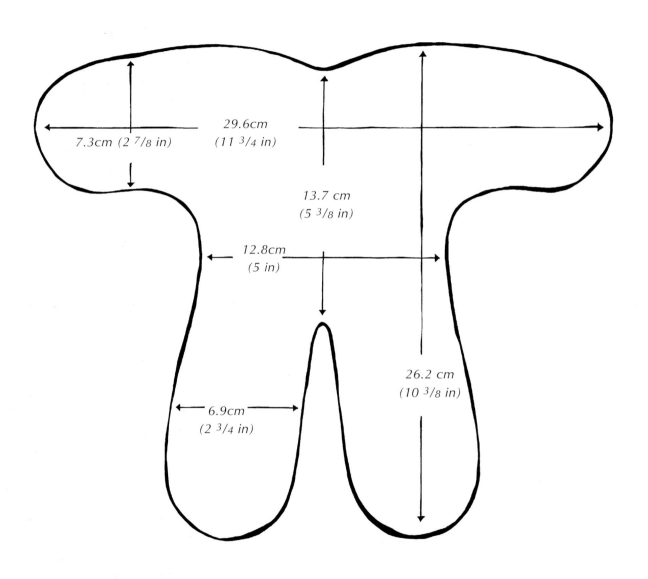

7.3cm (2 7/8 in)

29.6cm (11 3/4 in)

13.7 cm (5 3/8 in)

12.8cm (5 in)

6.9cm (2 3/4 in)

26.2 cm (10 3/8 in)

18.3 *Template for 'Doll with arms and legs'*

Doll with arms and legs

(Body: shaped felt; head: fully felted)

- Template (see figure 18.3), allowing for shrinkage
- 50 g (1 $^3/_4$ oz) wool for the body
- 50 g (1 $^3/_4$ oz) wool for the head; inner core
- 25 g (1 oz) leftover wool yarn; outer layer
- 25 g (1 oz) skin-coloured wool
- Approximately 5 g skin-coloured wool for the hands
- Some stuffing wool

Head
See 'Sack doll' page 75.

Body
Wind layers of wool completely around the template. It is best to use very long stapled wool. The tricky areas are the curves of the hands and feet, between the legs and the armpits. Holes and threadbare areas often develop in these places, so pay particular attention to them while layering the wool and felting it.

Cut a 5 cm (2 in) vertical slit into the back of the finished body.

Make pink hands for the doll, using approximately 2.5 g of wool. See 'Felting small balls' page 34.

Attaching the hands
Make an indentation at the end of the arm with your finger. Press the hand into this hollow and sew it on well enough that it remains in place.

Stuff the doll sparingly with wool. Do not stuff the top of the arms or legs or they will not be able to move later. Wind yarn around the ankles.

18.4   Doll with arms and legs

Once you have sewn up the slit at the back, felt the seam.

If desired, wind a length of yarn around the upper body to give it shape. Sew hair onto the head using satin stitch (mohair wool). This also hides the sewn cross at the crown from attaching the head. Hint at eyes and mouth. An invisible line connecting eyes and mouth should produce an equilateral triangle.

Note: Always finish the body while still damp, after spinning it in the washing machine. This allows you to shape it and place the arms and legs into a natural position for drying.

Only remove the thread around the head once the head is completely dry and has been attached to the body. It is best to make the head a few days in advance.

Small doll in a sleeping bag

(Shaped felt and felted balls)
- Oval cardboard template (see figure 18.6), allowing for shrinkage
- 30 g (1 oz) wool for the sleeping bag (half white, half coloured)
- Some skin-coloured wool for felting the head and hands
- Some thin yarn for knitting the body
- Set of 5 needles size 2.5 mm (12)

Sleeping bag

Wind the wool completely around the template: first the coloured, then the white layer. Once you have finished felting, cut a 4–5 cm (1 3/4–2 in) horizontal slit into the piece, as shown by the diagram figure 18.6, and turn inside out. Felt the coloured side and the cut edges again. To finish, only turn the head part of the sleeping bag back inside out. This makes a white pillow. Lightly full the whole piece over a washboard.

Head and hands

See 'Felting small balls' page 34.

Knitted body

Cast on 32 stitches in the round (8 stitches per needle). Rib 1 plain, 1 purl for 14 rows. Knit two stitches together for one row — each needle now has 4 stitches. Knit 8 rows, then pull the thread through all the stitches (neck). Cast on 8 stitches for each arm, knit 8 rows, cast off and sew together.

Stuff the chest with some wool. Fasten a thread securely to the chest with a needle, bring it up through the neck opening and right through the head. Then see 'Sack doll, Attaching the head' page 75.

Sew the hands onto the lightly stuffed arms with tiny stitches and attach the arms to the body. Lightly stuff the body and sew the seam shut at the base.

Hat

Crochet 5 chain stitches, close the circle and crochet 12 single crochet stitches around the circle until the hat is the correct size.

Before inserting the doll into the sleeping bag, attach a cord to hang it around a neck. This allows the child to take the doll everywhere while still having their hands free.

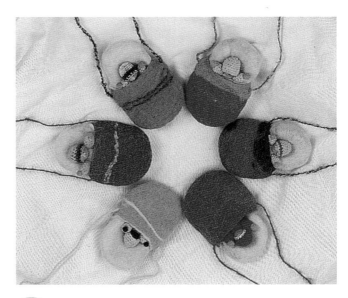

18.5 *Small dolls in sleeping bags*

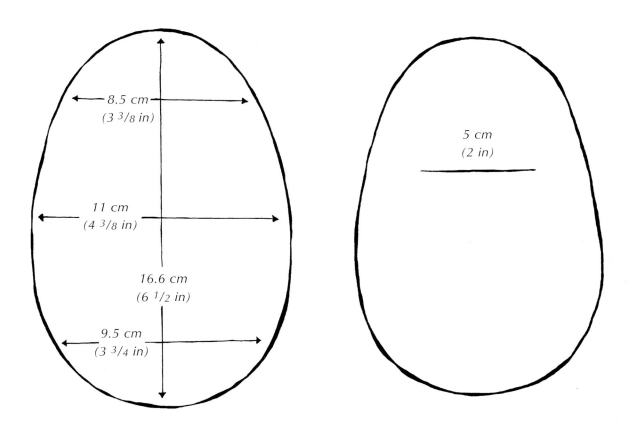

8.5 cm
(3 3/8 in)

11 cm
(4 3/8 in)

16.6 cm
(6 1/2 in)

9.5 cm
(3 3/4 in)

5 cm
(2 in)

Slit in the raw felt piece (approximate)

18.6 Template measurements for 'Small doll in sleeping bag'

18.7 *Doll's clothes made out of handmade felt*

Beautiful things for dolls

This doll girl is kitted out with a felt hat, waistcoat and shoes.

Hat
The pictured doll's head circumference is 36 cm (14 in), so 40 g (1 ¹/₂ oz) of wool is needed to make a hat. Make it according to the 'boy's hat with a feather' page 49.

Boots
The shoes in the photo each weigh 25 g (1 oz). They are made in the same way as the larger woollen boots on page 60. Naturally, it is not possible to felt the boots on the doll's feet. Instead, they are only shaped using the template.

Waistcoat
- For a doll's body length of 50 cm (20 in), you will need 50g (1 ³/4 oz) wool
- Cardboard template (figure 18.10), including shrinkage

Felt both front sides of the doll's waistcoat at the same time. To do this, wind the wool around the template and once felted, cut the felt apart around the edges. This makes two identical pieces, and saves work. The back is felted as a flat piece.

Sew the pieces together at the shoulders and side. Felt along the seams and the cut edges again. The pictured doll's waistcoat is fastened with a small wooden brooch.

Note: Waistcoats for children and adults can be made in the same way, using a suitably larger template.

18.8   *Dolls' hats*

18.9   *Dolls' boots*

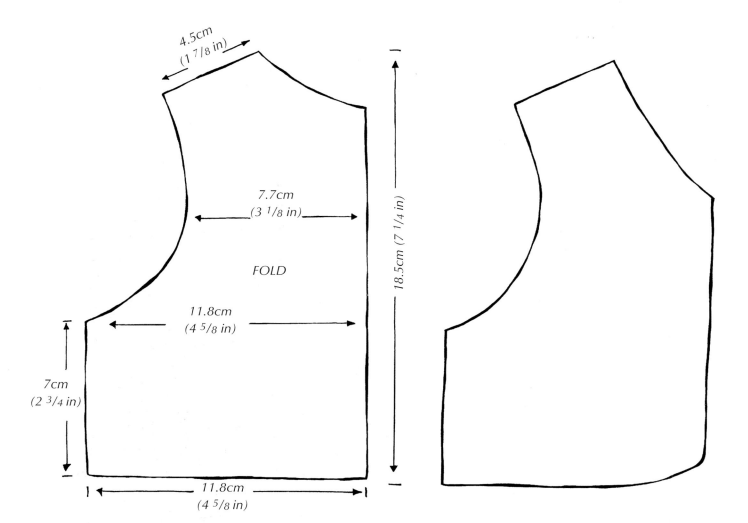

4.5cm
(1 7/8 in)

7.7cm
(3 1/8 in)

FOLD

18.5cm (7 1/4 in)

11.8cm
(4 5/8 in)

7cm
(2 3/4 in)

11.8cm
(4 5/8 in)

Back - felt as a flat piece

Front - wind around template and later cut open aroud the edges

18.10   *Template for doll's waistcoat*

'Birth of a doll'

It was Advent time.

A mother was making a simple sack doll out of cloth and wool. Through the door, she heard her small son saying to his younger sister, 'You can't go in there now, there's a doll being born.' The little sister did not say anything and did not ask about it over the next few days. But in the corner of her room, slightly hidden, she made a small bed out of pillows and blankets. She placed a biscuit on the pillow.

One morning the doll was finished. Its body was knitted out of plant-dyed wool, head and hands covered with cotton knit cloth, eyes and mouth only hinted at. A few strands of light mohair wool was the 'baby hair.'

The mother carried the doll into the children's room and placed it in the arms of the little child. Her face lit up, and her cheeks turned red with pleasure.

Now an exciting time started for both of them: the doll used a lot of nappies, learnt to talk and had chicken pox, like its mother too. It went on holidays and was even stung by a wasp once. Oh, it needed a lot of comforting, but at the same time it gave comfort.

And just because this doll was so simple — no eyes that shut, no inserted synthetic hair, no fixed expression on its face — the child could see anything in it: large and small, kind and angry, pale and red, as there was nothing to hinder the child's imagination.

85

Seasonal Toys — Spring

Spring fairy

(Modelled felt, flat felt, felt ball)

For reference: the pictured fairy weighs 20 g

- Different shades of blue and skin colour magic wool
- White unspun sheep's wool, approximately 30 x 25 cm (12 x 10 in)
- Tulle (fabric store)
- Small amount of white unspun silk or ramie for the hair
- Pipe cleaners (chenille stems)
- Sewing needle, thread, doll needle (extra long sewing needle)
- Blue and red sewing silk (for eyes and mouth)

19.2   *Spring fairy*

19.1   *Spring fairy*

- Blue and red coloured pencils.

Body

Bend the pipe cleaners into shape for the body (see diagram 19.3).

Open the loops at hands and feet and wrap skin coloured wool around them, then press back together (see figure 19.4).

Wind very thin layers around the arms and legs, including hands and feet. Wet each new layer with warm water and felt gently with soapy fingertips. Gently model the body: thin wrists and ankles, stronger upper arms and thighs (see figure 19.4).

Add layers of white wool to the body, model and felt.

Massage and stroke the small figure. Dip into warm water now and again, gently squeeze out excess water and felt with soapy fingers. Add small tufts of wool to calves, hips, shoulders, chest etc. where necessary, and carefully felt.

Continue working until you are satisfied with the figure. To finish, thoroughly rinse out the soap

19.4 *After winding wool around the loops, press them together again and wrap a thin layer around the hand, then felt*

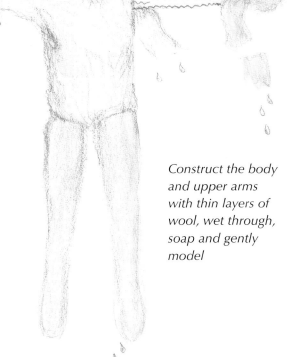

19.3 *Wire body (red = Inuit doll)*

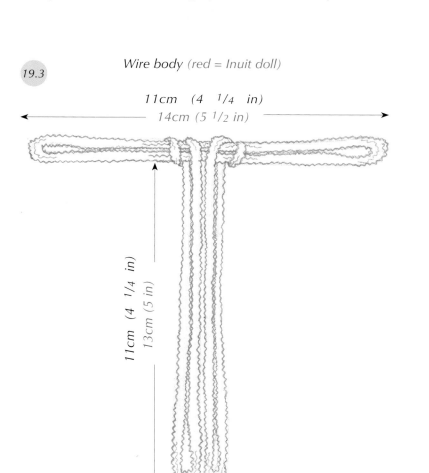

11cm (4 1/4 in)

14cm (5 1/2 in)

11cm (4 1/4 in)

13cm (5 in)

Construct the body and upper arms with thin layers of wool, wet through, soap and gently model

Make hands and legs using skin coloured wool as above

Head

Wind a small, skin-coloured ball, immerse in warm water, squeeze out lightly and roll gently between soapy palms. Roll more vigorously once the ball has started felting. The finished head should be the size of a hazelnut and not too soft.

Joining the head to the body: Place the head on the shoulders while head and body are still damp. Take a long doll needle threaded with a double thread. Make a knot at one end. Push the needle through the head from the top, and right through the body, coming out between the legs. Push the needle back in just beside this point and return the same way (see figure 19.5). Repeat this process a few times, pulling the thread tight. The head should sit firm and securely.

Place a bit of white wool between the legs and felt on to cover any visible stitches.

Make an elegant neck by winding some long fibre wool tightly between head and shoulders. Re-felt the neck.

Wings and garments

To make delicate but stable wings, felt on a piece of tulle. Different shades of blue produce a beautiful marbled effect.

Spread out a *very* thin layer of blue wool. Smooth the piece of tulle, about 30 x 25 cm (12 x 10 in), over it. Then add a second, very thin layer of blue wool.

Sprinkle warm water over the wool and gently rub with soapy hands. The two layers of wool will gradually penetrate through the holes in the tulle and felt together. This will take some time; continue felting patiently.

To finish, rinse well and then iron flat.

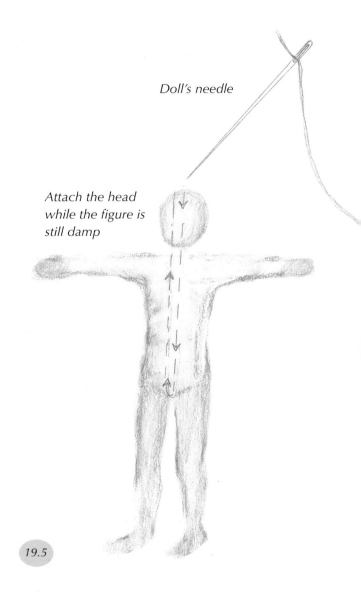

Doll's needle

Attach the head while the figure is still damp

19.5

Cut the wing and garment pattern (see figure 19.6) out of paper. Pin to the tulle and cut out. You now have both wings and the fairy garment in one.

Cut a strip, 15 x 5 cm (6 x 2 in), out of the remaining tulle. Wind this strip around the lower body of the fairy as an undergarment. Sew to the chest, back and under the arms. Gather the garment along the top edge between the points shown, fit it to the body and sew tight.

Sew the wings together, unfold and smooth the seam.

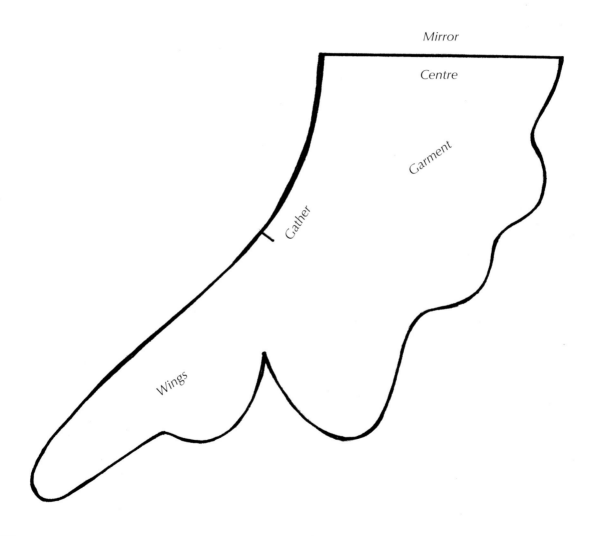

Mirror

Centre

Garment

Gather

Wings

19.6 *Wings and garments of the 'Spring fairy', full-scale pattern*

Shoes

Bend the feet into shape. Cut out two ovals, considerably larger than the feet, from the remaining piece of felted tulle. Run a gathering thread right around the edge of the oval, place the feet inside, pull the thread tight and sew in the ends. The shoes are finished.

If you would prefer boots, as shown in the illustration, cut two small strips of felted tulle, wind them around the ankles and sew them tight for the bootlegs.

Hat and hair

Felt a small thin disc between your palms using blue wool. Place the centre over your thumb and felt it into a hat shape.

Trim the brim if necessary, then fray the edges for a light and transparent look.

Sew the hat to the head while damp; do not position it too far down the face.

To make the hair, place a length of ramie or silk around the face, under the hat brim. Sew to the head at the crown and ears with a stitch respectively.

Face

Carefully draw eyes and mouth with a blue and red pencil. Make sure the eyes are not too high up; the fairy should have a high forehead and appear childlike.

Sew a tiny cross with blue silk thread over the blue eye dots and a small, horizontal satin stitch with red sewing silk over the red drawn mouth, pull tight. Draw the thread up from the neck, and sew the threads in at the neck.

To finish, shade cheeks with a red pencil.

To suspend, attach a thread to the back of the head and to the point where the wings join the body.

19.7   *Flying fairy*

90

Easter eggs

(Modelled felt — children can make these)

- Just under 10 g (¹/₃ oz) wool (for a hen-sized felt egg)

Wind the wool into a tight ball and immerse in warm water, then squeeze lightly.

Carefully roll between soapy hands. Once the surface has started felting, roll, squeeze and massage more vigorously until the ball is firm and even.

Smooth stripes, spots or a thin layer of different coloured wool over the ball for decoration. Felt on with your fingertips and then roll carefully between your hands.

Once the colours are sufficiently felted on, roll the ball firmly between your hands in a *single* direction to make an egg shape: one end pointy, the other round.

Continue massaging and modelling until you are satisfied with the result.

19.8   *Easter eggs*

19.9   *Five small rabbits*

Five small rabbits

(Modelled felt)
Make several of these small rabbits at the same time as they look best in a group. With some practice a rabbit takes about 20–30 minutes. They are made out of two felted eggs, a larger, hen sized egg for the body and a smaller egg for the head.

- Slightly more than 10 g (¹/₃ oz) white sheep's wool
- Some pink wool
- Needle, white sewing thread
- Dark blue embroidery thread
- Pink coloured pencil
- Thick needle with a large eye, doll needle

Make two eggs, one larger and one smaller, using most of the white wool (see 'Easter eggs' page 91). The remaining wool is for ears, front paws and the tail.

Assemble the rabbit while head and body are still damp.

Note: The pointy sides of the eggs are the chest and nose; make sure they are sewn together correctly.

Thread a double thread into the doll needle and make a knot at one end. Sew the head on tightly with several stitches, pushing the needle from the front paw area to the ears and back the same way. Ears and paws will later cover these stitches. Make sure the head is attached firmly to the body and does not wobble.

Ears

Thread a long, thick strand of wool through the needle with a large eye. Push the needle into the neck and emerge at the top of the head, between the forehead and back of the head. Push the needle back into the head just beside the point from where it emerged, leaving a loop about 3 cm (1 ½ in) long for the first ear.

Make the second ear in the same way just beside the first ear.

Let the remaining strand of wool end somewhere in the body.

Take a thinner, pink strand of wool and make a smaller loop in the same way at the front of each ear.

Front paws and tail

Thread a strand of wool into the needle with a large eye and make two small loops or loose stitches at the front of the chest for the front paws.

Make a small loop at the back for the tail.

How to felt the ears

Dip the rabbit into warm water ears first. Soap your fingers well and carefully massage and stroke each ear until the pink and white wool have felted together nicely and the ear is well connected to the head.

If the ears are too long, trim and re-felt the cut edges. If they are too thin, add on bits of wool and felt.

How to felt the paws

Wet the chest with warm water.

Add some bits of wool to the paw loops and gently press them in place with soapy fingers. Stroke and felt until the paws are nice and round and well connected to the chest.

Sit the rabbit down. If it tips over, add more wool to the paws and felt as described above.

Rinse the animal well and use a towel to squeeze out excess moisture.

Face

Sew a small cross for the eyes with dark blue embroidery thread. Pull the thread tight and do not make the stitches too large.

Draw a nose with a pink coloured pencil.

Note: Make sure the head is not too small in relation to the body. Set the ears far enough back in the head: the forehead should be beautifully round with sufficient space for the eyes. Embroider the eyes at the side of the head, closer to the nose than the ears.

19.10 *Easter nests*

Easter nests

(Shaped felt)
It is best to make two Easter nests out of a single template. This requires hardly any more work and will give you an extra Easter present!
- Green magic wool
- Cardboard for the circular template

Wind the green wool evenly and carefully around the circular template. Wet through, soap and felt.

Once well felted, cut in half and remove the cardboard.

Continue felting both nests, particularly the cut edges and inside.

To finish, fold back and shape a nice brim.

Note: Use sufficient wool to make the nests sturdy, without holes. Several shades of green make a more beautiful and interesting looking nest.

Large rabbit

(Modelled felt, shaped felt)

During Easter time, this solid wool-felted rabbit can carry a pannier on its back for Easter eggs. Throughout the rest of the year, it makes a lovely soft toy, which is suitable for small children.

Even an experienced felter will take approximately two days to make this toy. It is not a suitable project for felting beginners. Keep a picture or even a real rabbit nearby while working.

The rabbit pictured is 28 cm (11 in) high (seated, without ears) and weighs 250 g $^1/_2$ lb).

- Wool batt for the fur
- Pink wool for the inside of the ears
- Pink, dark brown and white leftover pieces of felt or embroidering thread for nose, mouth, eyes and teeth
- Cardboard
- Needle and thread

Tightly roll up a thick piece of wool batt, 40 g (1 $^1/_2$ oz), approximately 55 x 18 cm (21 $^1/_2$ x 7 in), from the shorter side. Completely immerse it in warm soapy water and squeeze out lightly.

Fold a long strip, approximately 60 cm (23 $^1/_2$ in) long, in half widthways (now 30 cm (11 $^3/_4$ in) long). Wet and felt it lightly to the top third of the roll, adding several thin layers of wool over the areas where it joins the body. Remember to leave a long enough piece of wool roll to make the head later. These are the front legs, each one approximately 9 cm (3 $^1/_2$ in) long.

Make the hind legs at the base of the roll in the same way, folding over a strip approximately 100 cm (39 $^1/_2$ in) long. Each hind leg should be approximately 12 cm (4 $^3/_4$ in) long.

19.11   Large rabbit

Turn the figure round. Wet and felt the front legs with several thin layers of wool. Then wind layers of wool lengthwise and cross-wise around the legs to build them up. Wet, add soap and squeeze the legs into a round roll.

Place the animal on its side. Add more bits of wool to the thighs and hind legs to make them

95

strong and round, stroking the wool out towards the backside. Remember that felting will make the legs a lot thinner. If necessary, lengthen the hind legs. Bend the hind legs upwards (see figure 19.15) and carefully massage the paws of the front legs downwards.

Pull out the base of the head slightly. Add plenty of thin layers and bits of wool to build up the head. Make the cheeks, nose and chin.

Note: only lightly felt the back and top of the head, as the ears still need to be attached.

Once the basic proportions are correct, carefully stroke and rub the figure, then massage with increasing vigour.

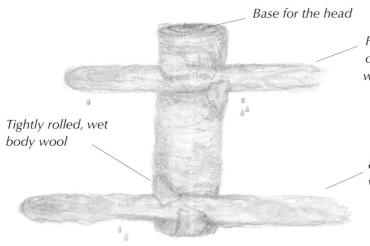

Base for the head

Fold a strip of wool in half, approximately 60 cm (23 1/2 in) long, and attach to the body with plenty of bits of wool (front legs)

Tightly rolled, wet body wool

80–100cm (31 1/2–39 1/2 in) long strip of wool, instructions see above (hind legs)

19.12   1. Attaching the legs to the back

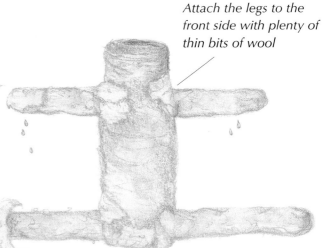

Attach the legs to the front side with plenty of thin bits of wool

Press the wet, soapy legs together like sausages. Wind thin layers of wool around all four limbs, lengthwise and crosswise, until the legs are long and thick enough.

19.13   2. Front side (turn the figure over)

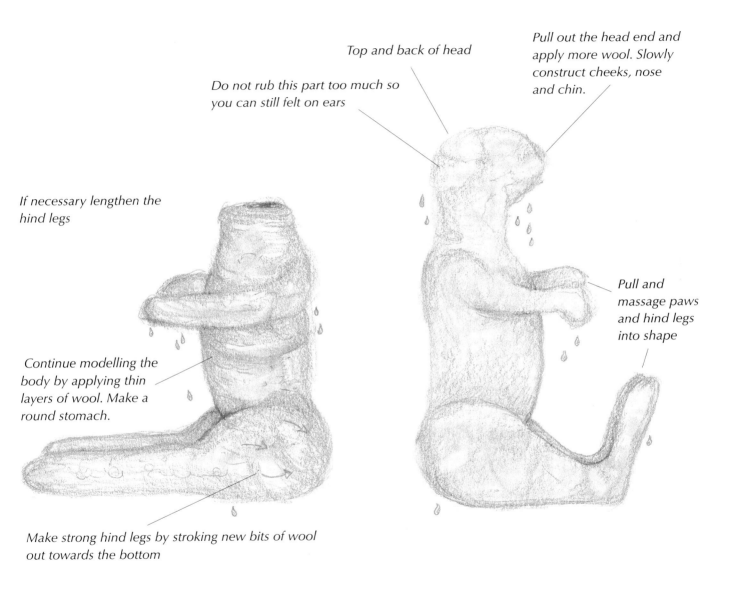

Top and back of head

Do not rub this part too much so you can still felt on ears

Pull out the head end and apply more wool. Slowly construct cheeks, nose and chin.

If necessary lengthen the hind legs

Pull and massage paws and hind legs into shape

Continue modelling the body by applying thin layers of wool. Make a round stomach.

Make strong hind legs by stroking new bits of wool out towards the bottom

19.14   3. Place the wet animal on its side.

19.15   4. Sit the rabbit down

Ears
(Shaped felt)

Cut two identical templates out of cardboard (see figure 19.16). Place a small amount of pink wool in the centre of the template. Wind layers of fur-coloured wool around the template, and felt lightly.

Cut a slit along the base. Remove the template, turn the ear right side out, smooth it flat and continue felting. Felt the top area more vigorously than the cut edges.

Sew the ears to the head with plenty of small stitches. Sew right around the cut edge, folding the ears together slightly at the base. The ears should not be too close together or too far into the forehead.

Place plenty of thin bits of wool onto the still soft base of the ears and head. Patiently and gently massage the area; simultaneously construct the back of the head.

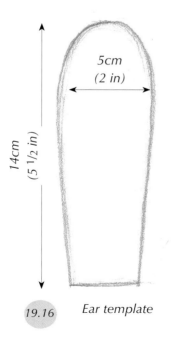

5cm
(2 in)

14cm
(5 1/2 in)

19.16   Ear template

Sew the felted ears to the head with plenty of small stitches. Re-felt the seams using thin bits of wool.

After attaching the ears, continue constructing the face and head: model the face, full the eye sockets, pull and push the nose out

Make su you hav nice nec line

Sew on a felted tuft of wool as a tail. the seams with bits of wool and felt.

19.17   5. Completion

Modelling the face

Felt and full two sockets at either side of the face for the eyes. Pull and push the nose out. Round the cheeks. Make sure the chin-neck line is in proportion. Felt the pre-felted eyes and nose into place. If necessary sew them tightly first with a few stitches, or alternatively embroider them on later.

Tail

Lightly felt a white tuft of wool, and sew it to the rabbit's bottom with plenty of small stitches. Place small bits of wool over the seam and felt.

Continue felting and working the animal from all sides, evenly and patiently, until you are happy with the results.

Shower the finished rabbit repeatedly with cold water to rinse out all the soap. Dry seated on a thick, folded towel.

Carrot: see 'Felted vegetables' page 104.

19.18   *Finished rabbit*

Seasonal Toys — Summer

Magic flower and flower child

(Modelled and shaped felt)

The wire loops felted within the petals allow you to open and shut this 'magic flower' around the flower child.

Placed at the child's bedside, it can become the highlight of a bedtime ritual. During the bedtime story or lullaby, leave the flower open. Then carefully shut it petal by petal, enveloping the flower child within. Open the flower again the next morning so the child can play with the flower doll throughout the day.

Magic flower and flower child

20.1

20.2

- Approximately 50 g (1 3/4 oz) coloured wool for the entire flower, mainly dark red and green
- Some skin-coloured and yellow wool
- Red and pink pipe cleaners (chenille stems)
- 1 spare wooden knitting needle or equivalent
- Blue and red sewing silk
- Blue and red coloured pencils
- Clay flowerpot

Bend the red pipe cleaners into seven identical teardrop shaped loops (see figure 20.3).

Wind several thin layers of red wool around the loops, wet and felt. Try not to bend the loops out of shape. Make sure the pipe cleaners are not visible through the wool. Do not felt around the ends of the loops; they will be used for making the stem later.

Once you have finished felting the petals, gather them together to make the flower and secure with a piece of thin wire.

20.3   *Loops*

Twist the pipe cleaner ends together tightly to make the flower stem. This also makes the flower head more stable.

Green leaves

For instructions on how to make leaves, see 'Leaf bags' page 108.

Use green wool and make the leaves a suitable size for your flower. After felting, cut open around the entire edge to make two beautifully veined leaves. Re-felt the cut edges!

Simpler version: Felt a green wool sheet and cut out two leaves with a small leaf stalk. Re-felt the cut edges!

Felt the stem right up to the petals using green wool. Felt in the leaf stems. Sew them to the stalk if necessary with a few stitches first. If the petals are loose, sew them tightly with a needle and thread.

Shape a flat calyx (sepals) around the underside of the petals and felt.

Make a round cushion with yellow wool and sew it to the centre of the flower. Do not felt.

To strengthen the stem, push the knitting needle from below right through the green felt tube up to the petals.

Now 'plant' the flower in a pot: place polystyrene or similar material into a clay pot, drill a hole for the stem. Cover the surface with brown wool.

Flower child

(Modelled felt, shaped felt, felt ball)
The finished flower child weighs about 10 g (1/3 oz). For instructions on how to make the doll, see 'Spring fairy' page 86.

Bend the pipe cleaners into the body shape (see figure 20.5). See 'Spring fairy' page 86 for details on how to felt the arms and legs.

Felt the body, sleeves and short trousers using red wool.

Cap

Felt some yellow wool around a half circle cardboard template (see figure 20.4). Slit the base open, fit to the head and sew tight.

Shoes

Cut soles out of cardboard (see figure 20.4). Layer green wool around them and felt. Cut a slit into the top, insert the feet and sew tight.

Alternatively, run a gathering stitch around the hole to make shoes that can be removed.

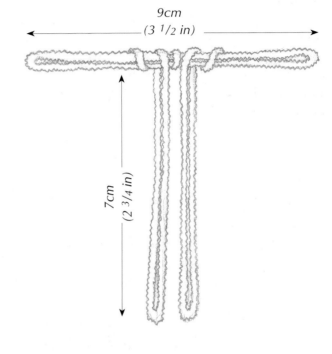

9cm
(3 ¹/₂ in)

7cm
(2 ³/₄ in)

Cardboard template for flower child cap. Full-scale pattern.

Shoe template for flower child. Full-scale pattern.

20.4

20.5   *Flower child (and mushroom gnome) wire body*

Felted vegetables

(Felted balls, modelled felt, flat felt)
These 'vegetables' are extremely hard-wearing and make good produce for a play shop. You can also use them for a teddy bears' picnic too (see page 142).

Cucumbers

Cut a long, curved cucumber shape out of cardboard, slightly smaller than the desired size of the finished cucumber. Wind layers of green wool around the cardboard. Immerse the entire cucumber in warm water and gently felt with soapy hands.

The centre of the cucumber should be thicker than the ends. Continue felting until the miniature cucumber looks authentic and is firm and solid.

Rinse well. Leave the cardboard inside for added stability.

Oranges

Make a small ball with orange wool. Completely immerse it in hot water and squeeze out lightly. Roll and massage it between soapy hands, initially very gently and then more vigorously. Sew stem and base with green embroidery thread.

20.6　　*Felted vegetables*

Tomatoes

Follow the instructions for 'oranges', but use red wool and make them slightly smaller.

Melons

(Layered felt ball)

You will need dark green, red, pink and white wool.

First lightly felt a red ball, diameter approximately 5 cm (2 in).

Add a thin layer of pink wool to the red ball and felt on lightly. Then felt on a thin white layer and to finish a layer of dark green wool.

Make sure all the layers are wound very evenly. Roll and massage the ball extensively. Once the surface is well felted, work with a lot of strength. It is better for your hands if someone can help you at this stage!

Full the well-felted ball vigorously over a wash board or similar ridged surface, dipping it in hot water and squeezing it out in between. The longer and stronger you felt, the firmer the cut-open melon will be.

To finish, add the melon to the next 60°C (140°F) washing machine cycle to further firm the felt.

Cut the small melon open with a sharp knife to reveal the red fleshy centre. You can draw on seeds with a black felt tip pen.

Carrots

Wind a small sausage using orange — yellow wool. Wind a green piece of wool around one end.

Briefly immerse the whole carrot in hot water and place it on your soapy palm. Roll and massage the cylinder with the fingers of your other hand until it resembles a typical carrot shape.

Only felt the base of the green end well to connect it to the carrot; leave the tip lightly felted.

Lettuce

Felt two circles, one large and one smaller, between the palms of your hands, using several shades of green. The larger circle should cover your entire palm. The colours can be irregular, but should not be too thick.

Shape and felt a small ball using light green. This is the centre of the lettuce; a few 'creases' in the ball make it appear more realistic.

Place the two finished circles of felt on top of each other, the smaller one on the inside. With needle and green thread, run a gathering thread around the edge of each layer and pull together slightly. Place the light green ball into the hollow centre and attach with a few stitches.

Pull the lettuce leaves into shape – finished!

Mushrooms

(Shaped felt, ball)

Felt a white ball, see 'Oranges' page 103. Roll the ball energetically in one direction to make a small barrel shape.

To make the mushroom cap, see 'Mushroom gnome' page 106.

Sew the cap to the stalk and re-felt the seam.

Rub the base over a flat surface several times so the mushroom can stand well.

Butterflies

(Flat felt on tulle)
- Coloured wool
- A piece of tulle (from a fabric store)
- Brown length of long staple wool or lightly spun yarn for the body

For instructions on how to felt on tulle, see 'Spring fairy' page 86.

Cut the shape of a butterfly out of the felted tulle, either following the pattern (see figure 20.8) or using your own shape.

Fold the wings in half, with the inside of the wings facing outwards.

Sew a length of long staple wool or yarn, approximately 10 cm (4 in) long, to the fold with a few stitches.

Divide one side of overhanging wool into two strands and tie a knot at each end for feelers.

To suspend, sew a length of thread to the base of the top wing.

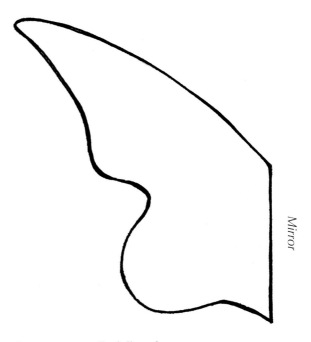

Mirror

20.8   *Butterfly full-scale pattern*

Butterflies with 'Spring fairy' p 86.

20.7

105

Seasonal Toys — Autumn

Mushroom gnome

(Modelled felt, shaped felt, felt ball)
A little group of mushroom gnomes look very nice seated together and look fantastic on a harvest festival table. You can either surround them with different autumn plants, or hide them in soft moss with only their mushroom caps peeking out. Children particularly enjoy 'picking' these mushrooms to take a closer look!

The finished figure weighs approximately 20 g (3/4 oz).

- Light brown, dark brown, white and green wool
- Pipe cleaners (chenille stems)
- Brown and red sewing silk
- Pink coloured pencil
- Some thin but firm cardboard

Bend the pipe cleaners for the body (see diagram page 32). Use natural white wool for the arms, hands, legs and feet. For further instructions, see 'Spring fairy' page 86.

Felt the head slightly larger than the spring fairy's head. Sew the head further down towards the chest rather than directly on top of the

21.1   *Mushroom gnomes snoozing in the moss*

shoulders like for the doll; this gives the gnome a slight hunchback. For further instructions, see 'Spring fairy' (but do not make a neck).

Shoes

Using dark green wool, felt around the sole template (see figure 21.2). For further instructions, see 'Flower child' page 101. Make the feet and shoes larger so the gnomes can stand securely.

Mushroom cap

The diameter of the pictured caps is 6–8 cm (2 1/4–3 1/8 in).

Cut the cap template out of cardboard (see figure 21.2).

Place mushroom-coloured wool over one side, smooth the wool over the edges and wet well.

Turn the template over, cover the other side with white wool. Wet, soap and felt. Once well felted, cut a small slit into the centre of the white side. Remove the cardboard, turn the mushroom cap right side out and continue felting.

Fit the cap to the head and sew on with several stitches. Do not push the hat too far down the face.

Making the face

Sew two small, slightly slanted satin stitches for the eyes and a red satin stitch for the mouth. If you want, shade the cheeks with a red coloured pencil.

Cardboard template for mushroom cap

Cut a small slit into the white side of the finished cap

21.3   *Gnomes' caps*

21.2   *Mushroom gnome shoe template*

Leaf bag

(Shaped felt)

Colourful autumn leaves, swirling through the air, have inspired these unique leaf bags. If you attach a leather strap to the leaf stalk, you can hang the bag around your neck or fasten it to your belt, giving you a beautiful and distinctive autumn bag.

- Approximately 50 g (1 ³/4 oz) wool for a leaf approximately 30 x 20 cm (11 ³/4 x 8 in)
- Cardboard and pencil

21.4 *Reverse side of leaf bag (shown on right)*

Draw the outline of your leaf on the cardboard, adding approximately 2 cm (³/4 in) all around for shrinkage. Cut out your template.

Place leaf veins over the template using long staple wool. Wet strands are easier to put exactly in place. Choose a colour for the veins that contrasts well with the leaf colour. You can also add small bits of different colours for a mottled effect.

Place thin, even layers of leaf-coloured wool over the template. Wet the wool after each layer.

Once finished, carefully press the wool down with the flat of your soapy palm and rub gently for 2–3 minutes. Turn the template over.

Smooth the overhanging leaf veins around the edges to make veins on the other side; if necessary add new strands of wool.

Now smooth the rest of the wet wool around the edges. Make the other side of the leaf in the same way, carefully smooth the overhanging wool around the edges, then felt.

Once the leaf has felted sufficiently, cut a small horizontal slit into the lower third of one side (stalk end), remove the template, turn the leaf right side out and view your handiwork!

Felt this outer side, put your hand inside the form and shape the tips of the leaf and the stalk well.

Note: If you make one side more beautiful, do not cut into it. Mark the other, less beautiful side with small different coloured tufts of wool whilst applying the layers, so you know which side to cut into.

21.5 *Leaf bags*

21.6 *Leaf bags*

Seasonal Toys — Winter

Star music box

(Shaped felt)
Star size: approximately 26 cm (10 in) diameter, measured from point to point.

- You will need a music box with a pull string (from craft or toy shop). Buy the music box first so you can adapt the star size to fit it if necessary.
- Approximately 40 g (1 $^1/_2$ oz) light yellow wool
- Approximately 40 g (1 $^1/_2$ oz) stuffing wool
- Cardboard
- Needle and thread

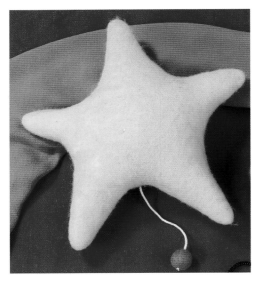

22.1 *Star music box*

Cut a five-pointed star out of cardboard and round off the points. Wind yellow wool around it in layers. Wet each layer and press down.

Pay special attention to star points and grooves, the wool tends to slip or bunch in these places. The star needs to be strong, so felt from all sides extensively.

Cut a slit into the back, just long enough for the music box to fit through. Turn the star right side out.

Thoroughly felt each point again. Push your finger inside the star and work the points, twisting and felting them over your fingertip until they are clear and distinct.

Once dry, stuff the points. Then insert the music box through the slit into the star and stuff wool around it.

Sew the seam shut. Attach a cord for hanging up.

Note: Sew the music box into a tight cloth bag. Cut a small disc out of firm cardboard and make a small slit from the edge to the centre. Make a small hole in the centre with a sharp object. Slip the music box string along the slit to the hole in the centre. Push the disc right up to the music box. This stops wool fibres from being pulled into the music box when the cord retracts.

Santa Claus boot

(Shaped felt)

- Approximately 35 g (1 ¼ oz) dark red wool
- Approximately 30 g (1 oz) white wool
- Some yellow wool
- Cardboard

Cut the boot template out of cardboard (see figure 22.2).

Felt a flat yellow sheet. Cut small stars out of it, using a star cookie cutter or equivalent pattern. Dip the stars into warm water and place them evenly over one side of the template. Lay thin layers of red wool over the template and stars, wet thoroughly, and carefully felt. Turn the template over. Spread stars over the other side of the template in the same way.

Now smooth the overhanging wet red wool around the side of the template over the new stars. Lay down new layers of red wool as described above, until the red wool is used up completely.

Place the white wool over the boot in the same way for the inner surface, until the entire boot is tightly packed in wool. Felt extensively. Full the boot over a washboard or a ridged draining board.

Cut open along the top, remove the cardboard and turn right side out. Continue felting the outer surface with the stars. Slip one hand into the boot and shape, working the edges and massaging away any bulges. Full the sole of the boot over the washboard.

Once dry, turn back the bootleg a few centimetres to reveal the white inside.

Attach a string for hanging up.

Note: You can also felt the boot on a child's foot once the template has been removed.

If you want to felt a pair of boots, make them both at the same time using a single template, joined together at the bootleg. You will need double the amount of wool.

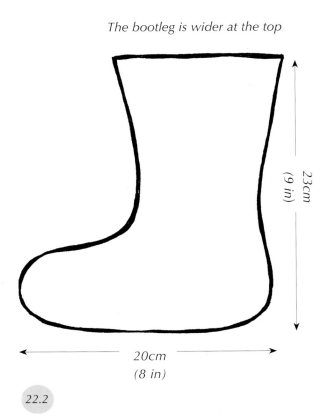

The bootleg is wider at the top

23cm
(9 in)

20cm
(8 in)

22.2

The boot and Christmas tree hide sweet treats

Hollow Christmas tree

(Shaped felt)

This distinctive tree makes a great advent or Christmas present as it looks very decorative and can be filled with all sorts of delicious things! See page 108 for a view of the reverse side.

- 60 g (2 oz) dark green wool
- Some brown wool
- Cardboard
- Tree decorations: yellow, red, violet and white wool; white pipe cleaners; some yellow and red glass beads; thin gold wire or thread

Cut a fir tree out of cardboard according to the measurements given in the diagram (see figure 22.4).

Layer green wool over the template, wet through and press down.

Once the tree (without trunk) is completely covered in green wool, wind brown wool around the trunk. It should overlap the green wool by approximately 1–2 cm (3/4 in).

Note: Make sure there are no holes or bulges at the points and grooves as the wool tends to pull apart or bunch up in these tricky areas. Add new bits of wool if necessary.

Once felted, cut a horizontal slit approximately 8 cm (3 in) long into the upper third of the tree. Turn right side out.

Shape the points by twisting and felting them over your finger. Push green wool from the inside into holes or thin areas and felt in place.

Christmas tree decorations
- *Stars*: Felt a yellow flat sheet, cut out stars, and sew to the tree with a stitch in the centre and a bead.

- *Apples:* Make red felt balls (see page 34), head of 'Spring fairy' page 86, or 'Oranges' page 103.
- *Pine cones:* Felt soft small balls using violet wool, then roll them vigorously between the palms of your hands in a single direction to make a cone shape. Attach to the tree with a stitch at the top and a red bead.
- *Candy cane:* Lightly felt white wool around a pipe cleaner. Pull out very thin lengths of red, long staple wool and wind around the cane. Felt lightly. Cut the wire into 5 cm (2 in) pieces. Bend the top part into a curve. Sew to the tree.

Use gold wire or thread to further decorate the tree. Attach a loop to the top of the tree to hang it up.

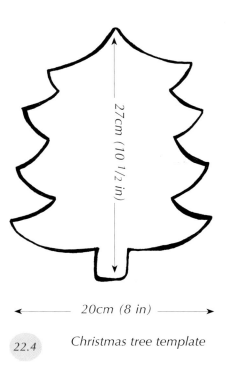

27cm (10 1/2 in)

20cm (8 in)

22.4   *Christmas tree template*

113

Igloo

Igloo

(Shaped felt, flat felt)
It will take 2–3 days to make an igloo. To stop your hands from getting sore, ask someone to help you with the felting.

- Approximately 200 g (7 oz) white wool
- Needle and thread
- A large piece of cardboard

Make a thick felt sheet using approximately half the wool. Cut it into small squares. Wet the squares and place half of them side by side on one side of the cardboard template for 'blocks of ice' (see figure 22.6). Layer half of the remaining wool over them and felt.

Turn the template over and arrange the remaining felt squares over the template. Carefully smooth the wet overhanging wool from the other side over to this side of the template. Layer on the remaining wool and felt.

Turn the template over again, smooth the wool over the sides as before, and felt. Minimum felting time: 1 hour.

Cut a slit along the base, remove the template, turn the igloo right side out, rinse and squeeze out well.

In most cases, not all of the ice blocks are sufficiently felted onto the background; sew loose blocks in place with a needle and thread.

Felt the outer side extensively. If necessary, cut along the lower edge again and re-felt the cut edges so the igloo can stand securely.

Cut an entrance into the igloo. If you want a more attractive entrance, felt a thick white sausage, sew it around the doorway and felt it on.

Note: To make a nice round shape, felt the igloo over a ball or similar round object for the last stages.

Felt until you are satisfied with the results. Rinse out well and spin in the washing machine.

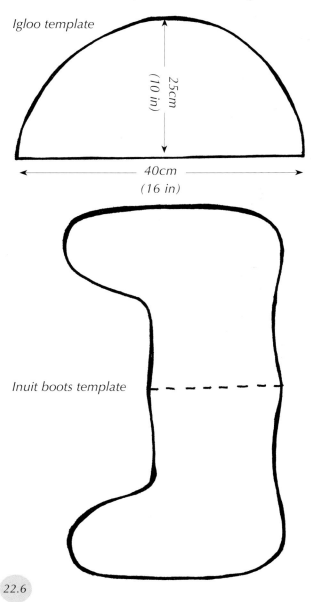

Igloo template

25cm
(10 in)

40cm
(16 in)

Inuit boots template

22.6

115

Inuit dolls

(Modelled felt, shaped felt)
You will need a whole day to make a doll plus
anorak and boots.
- Approximately 25 g (1 oz) coloured
wool: white, skin colour and black
- Pipe cleaners from a craft store
- *Face:* Red and black sewing silk or thin
embroidery thread; red and dark brown
coloured pencils
- *Anorak and boots:* Approximately 15 g
(1/2 oz) natural grey and white wool (light grey
wool mixed with a few dark brown streaks
looks surprisingly similar to seal fur); a strip of
real fur or a thick strip of felt
- *Jewellery:* different coloured, thin strands
of wool

For instructions on how to make the doll,
how to attach the head and a diagram sketch for
making the body out of pipe cleaners, see 'Spring
fairy' page 86.

Note: The head of the Inuit doll should be 9 cm
(3 1/2 in) circumference once finished, larger than
the Spring fairy's head.

Make smaller Inuit dolls for the children.

Hair (two wigs at once)

Cut a small disc out of cardboard, a little larger
than the circumference of the head. Sparsely
cover it in layers of black wool. Felt between the
palms of your hands.

Cut it in half and the 'raw wigs' are finished.
Continue to shape or cut as necessary and sew to
the head.

22.7   *The Inuit dolls can be dressed and undressed*

Face

Wait until the head is completely dry before making the face.

Draw slightly slanting eyes with the brown coloured pencil. Sew a tight satin stitch over the drawn eyes using black thread. Draw the mouth with a red pencil and sew a tight satin stitch with red thread as described above. Shade cheeks with a red pencil.

Swaddling baby

Sparsely cover the small oval template (see figure 22.8) with grey wool and felt between your palms. Cut a small slit into the upper third of the wool as shown, remove the cardboard and rinse. Make a firm ball out of skin-coloured wool. Place the head into the slit and sew tight. If you want, sew eyes and mouth with silk thread and place a length of white yarn around the hood.

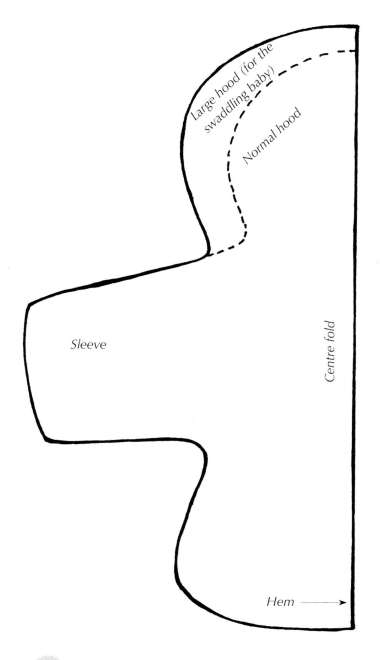

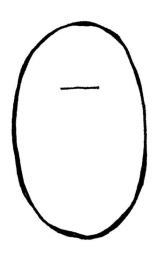

22.8   *Swaddling baby template*

22.9   *Inuit anorak (adult) template*

Anorak

Cut the template (figure 22.9) out of cardboard.

Note: Use the larger measurements for the hood if you want it to contain the swaddled baby.

Wet thin, coloured wool strands and wind them around the template for a decorative stripe. Wind grey wool in layers over the template, and wet through. To finish, layer white wool around the template. You will need approximately 10 g (1/3 oz) of wool for an entire anorak. Felt.

Cut open at the sleeves and hem, turn right side out and remove the cardboard. Cut a hole in the hood for the face. Careful! Do not make the hole too large as it will expand while felting.

Re-felt the outer side of the anorak and the cut edges.

If desired, sew a thin strip of fur to the hood and hem as trimming. The anoraks pictured have rabbit fur trimmings, clipped slightly. You can also make a 'fur' trimming using a thin felted sausage (see 'Felt cords' page 36) or a length of leftover felt.

Boots

Cut out a cardboard template (see figure 22.6). Both boots are made with one template connected at the bootleg; this saves work and ensures the boots are identical.

To make a coloured stripe along the base of the boot, wet two pieces of long staple wool and place them horizontally around the soles from heel to toe.

Wind grey or white wool in layers around the boots and felt.

Cut the bootlegs in half, remove the cardboard, turn right side out and shape.

Pull the boots on the doll while still wet. Wind a thread tightly around the ankle. Remove the thread after a few days. This gives them a better fit and a more elegant shape.

Note: Make the anorak and boots smaller to fit the doll children; remember the child's boots will be too small to turn right side out.

22.10   *Finished Inuit dolls*

Polar bear

(Modelled felt)
While felting the polar bear it is helpful to look at photos of live polar bears.

- Approximately 130 g (4 1/2 oz) white wool batt

Body

Tear off a piece of wool batt approximately 17 x 10 cm (6 3/4 x 4 in) long. Roll it up tightly from the narrow side, dip it in warm water and add soap.

Legs

Take two strips of wool batt (approximately 45 x 4 cm (18 x 1 1/2 in) and fold in half across the width to give you two loops. Place one strip (loop) at the base of the body roll (back legs). Place the second strip at the centre of the body (front legs). See figure 22.11.

Wet the legs and press them together. They should now be approximately 10 cm (4 in) long.

Smooth several wet bits of wool batt over the places where the legs meet the body to connect them to the body (see figure 22.11). Lay the animal down on its side.

Strengthen the tops of the legs by applying several thin layers of wool, stroking gently and pressing the wool down with soapy fingers. Add several layers of wool to make a strong bear bottom, smoothing downwards from the sides of the back towards the backside.

Polar bear legs are strong and not too short. Apply bits of wool lengthwise and crosswise to build them up. Work at the areas where the legs meet the body particularly carefully.

Note: Make the front legs slightly shorter than the back legs.

Slowly construct the body using plenty of wool layers.

Make the chest, neck and head. Depending on whether you want the bear to be looking at the ground or in the air, massage the wool in the corresponding direction (see figure 22.12).

Stand the bear on its legs and look at it from all sides; if necessary, correct the shape. The bottom should be round and high, the shoulders pronounced, head and neck long and thin.

Ears

Gently pull the ears out of the head (before it has been felted too firmly) and felt them into shape. Position them towards the back of the head and quite far apart. They should be small, round and quite thick (see figure 22.13).

Tail

Polar bear tails are short and stumpy. Gently pull some wool out of the body (before it is well felted), add another bit of wool to it and felt.

Stroke, massage and gently press the figure until you are happy with its shape and all the wool has been used up.

Shower to rinse. The soapy water will run out through the paws.

Dry the bear standing upright on a folded towel. Never squeeze or spin it!

If you want a more detailed Inuit setting, you can make sledge dogs, seals, penguins, fish etc. For snow, spread out a large piece of white wool batt.

Step by step instructions for the polar bear

All four legs: Fold two long strands of wool together (loops). Smooth to the body with wet bits of wool batt.

22.11   1. Attaching the legs (front side)

Make the bear an ample bottom by stroking bits of wool over the side of the back towards the backside

Pull out the head and neck slightly, covering it with plenty of layers of wool

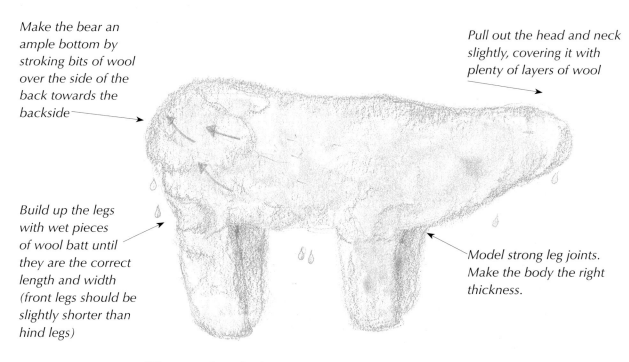

Build up the legs with wet pieces of wool batt until they are the correct length and width (front legs should be slightly shorter than hind legs)

Model strong leg joints. Make the body the right thickness.

22.12   2. Place the figure on its side (then change sides)

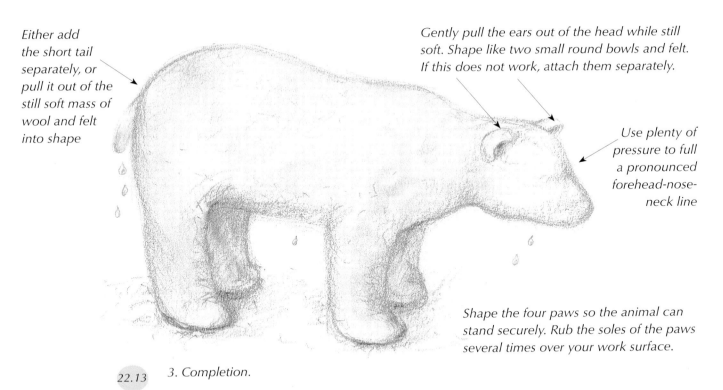

Either add the short tail separately, or pull it out of the still soft mass of wool and felt into shape

Gently pull the ears out of the head while still soft. Shape like two small round bowls and felt. If this does not work, attach them separately.

Use plenty of pressure to full a pronounced forehead-nose-neck line

Shape the four paws so the animal can stand securely. Rub the soles of the paws several times over your work surface.

22.13 3. Completion.

Dressing up

Dressing up does not need to be limited to parties. These woollen hats will keep children's heads nice and warm on a winter's day, and children like to slip into different roles throughout the year. Instructions for three animal hats are given here: a dog, a rabbit and a cockerel. The basic forms are the same shape, use the same amount of wool and can form the basis for different animal hats. Once you know the basics you can create any animal you wish. It is great fun and well worth experimenting!

23.1

Dog hat

(Shaped felt, flat felt)

- Approximately 90 g (3 ¹/₄ oz) dark brown wool (50 g for the cap, 40 g for *both* ears)
- Needle and thread
- Cardboard

Cut the template out of cardboard (see figure 23.2). Wind 50 g of wool around it in layers and felt.

Cut a slit along the base, remove the template and turn the felt right side out. The cap will still be far too large, so continue felting from all sides and full over a washing board or other ridged surface. Pay particular attention to the areas felted over the template edges. Any bulges need to be massaged away.

Fit the cap to the child's head; let them wear a bathing cap and massage the wool cap over it until it fits. Rinse well and squeeze out excess water.

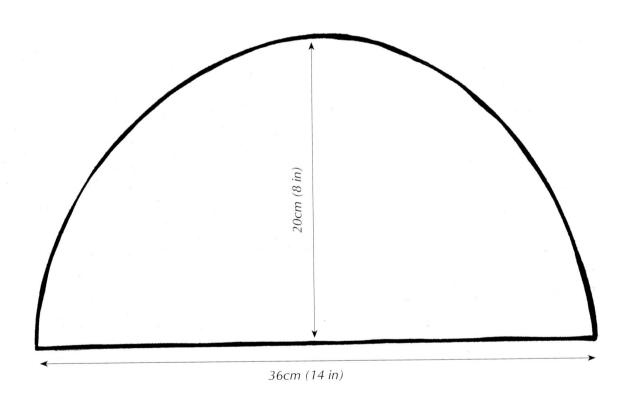

20cm (8 in)

36cm (14 in)

23.2   *Basic shape of the cap for dog, rabbit and cockerel*

Ears

Make a flat felt sheet using approximately 40 g (1 1/2 oz) of wool; make it approximately 4 mm (1/4 in) thick when finished, but only just large enough to cut out both ears. Cut the ears out following the template (see figure 23.3). Re-felt the cut edges and rinse.

Put the cap on to determine where to position the ears. Sew the ears to the cap from the underside of the ears; this makes them nice and bouncy. Felt small bits of wool to this area for a more pronounced lift and to cover the seam. If the new patch does not felt on well, sew it tight with a few stitches and then re-felt.

You can felt a tail for the dog. Attach a string for tying in place. Paint the child's nose brown!

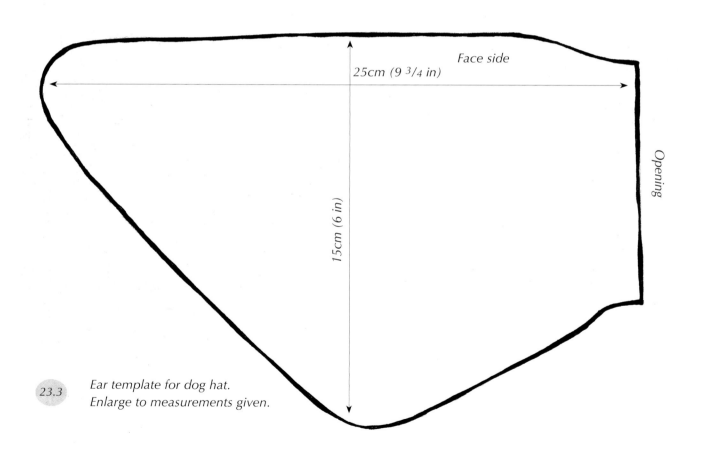

25cm (9 3/4 in)

Face side

Opening

15cm (6 in)

23.3 Ear template for dog hat.
Enlarge to measurements given.

23.4   *Dog hat*

Rabbit hat

(Shaped felt, felted wire, lightly felted ball)
- 125 g (4 1/2 oz) white wool (50 g for the cap, 60 g for *both* ears, 15 g for the tail)
- Pink wool (insides of the ears)
- Cardboard
- Needle and thread
- White pipe cleaners (chenille stems)
- Per ear you will need a piece of wire 70–80 cm (27 1/2 –31 1/2 in) long. Pipe cleaners are usually only 50 cm (19 3/4 in) long, but you could twist two together

To make the cap, see 'Dog hat' page 123 and figure 23.2

Cut out two identical templates for the ears (see figure 23.5). Lightly felt a flat sheet using pink wool and cut out two strips, 30 x 6 cm (11 3/4 x 2 3/8 in); round off the tips.

Wet the pink pieces and place them on the ear template. Layer white wool on top and felt well.

To attach the wires, bend each one into the exact shape of the ear and sew it around the felted ear (see diagram figure 23.6). The wire should stick out several centimetres at the base of the ear. Now you can remove the cardboard template. Carefully turn the ear right side out and smooth into shape. The wire inside the ear both stabilizes the ear and allows you to bend it into any position. Continue felting the outer side and pink strips.

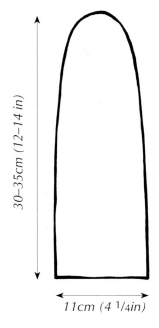

30–35cm (12–14 in)

11cm (4 1/4in)

23.5   Ears for the rabbit hat

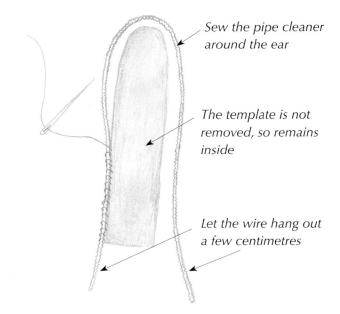

Sew the pipe cleaner around the ear

The template is not removed, so remains inside

Let the wire hang out a few centimetres

23.6   Rabbit hat. Reinforcing the ears.

Put the cap on to determine where to position the ears and mark the place. If the ears are too long you can cut them shorter. Fold the base of the ears into a small triangle. Cut a matching triangle into the cap at the place marked, push the ears into this hole and sew them to the cap from the inside, right around the base, with small stitches. If necessary sew them to the outer side of the cap too. Re-felt the seams. Bend back the wires on the inside of the cap and sew them tight.

Tail

Make a ball using 15 g (1/2 oz) of white wool. Dip it in warm water and felt it lightly between soapy hands. When needed, attach it to the child's trousers with a safety pin or a string

If you want you can paint the child's nose pink and purchase rabbit teeth from a toy shop.

Felt a carrot (see 'Felted vegetables' page 103) to hang around the child's neck.

23.7   *Rabbit hat*

Cockerel

(Shaped felt, felted cord, modelled felt)
- 50 g reddish brown wool for the cap
- Some coloured bits of wool for the feathers
- Slightly less than 50 g red wool for the comb
- Nearly 20 g yellow wool and a long staple, dark brown strand for the beak
- Cardboard
- Needle and thread
- Ribbon

Making the cap

Cut the template out of cardboard (see figure 23.2). Shape the coloured bits of wool into feathers, dip them briefly into water and spread them over the template.

Layer the reddish brown wool over the template and then see 'Dog hat' page 123 for further instructions.

Comb

Felt a thick cord, approximately 120 cm (48 in) long, out of red wool. Sew continuous loops along the centre line of the cap using the red cord; this is the base of the comb. Lay red bits of wool around each loop and felt between fingers and palms. Stand the cap on a thick terry towel to do this. If there are any gaps between the comb and the cap, sew the comb to the cap from the left and right with small stitches and then re-felt.

Beak

Place the thin, dark brown, wet wool strand along the centre of the template to the tip, to show the beak opening. Layer yellow wool over the template and felt.

Note: Make sure the brown stripe does not slip.

Cut open the wide side of the beak, remove the cardboard, turn right side out and continue felting. Press the beak together to make the brown line lie along the fold line and continue felting.

Felt the beak's edges to fit the child's face, particularly around the nose. If necessary, re-felt the cut edges. After shaping the beak let it dry.

Make nostrils with a wet coloured pencil and attach a ribbon to tie the beak in place.

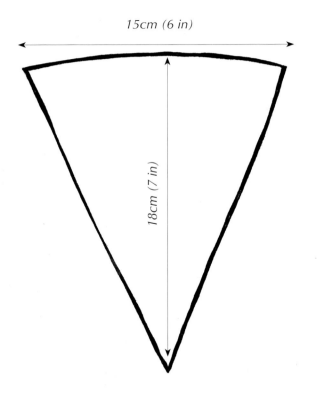

15cm (6 in)

18cm (7 in)

23.8   *Template for cockerel beak*

23.9   *Cockerel hat*

More ideas

Juggling balls

(Shaped felt)

- Make round cardboard discs for tem
  plates: 8–10 cm (3 ¹/₄–4 in) for children,
  allowing for shrinkage; 11–12 cm (4
  ¹/₂–4 ³/₄ in) for larger hands, allowing for
  shrinkage
- 20–25 g (³/₄–1 oz) wool (inside white,
  outside coloured)
- Millet or rice for stuffing

Place the wool evenly around the small
cardboard disc.

Note: The layers of wool easily slip apart
around the edges, and are usually too thick in the
centre. It is particularly important that juggling
balls are felted intensely and for a long time.
Firstly, because the opening slit should only be
small enough to remove the cardboard, but not to
turn the ball inside out to felt the inside; secondly,
a juggling ball has to survive a fair amount of
wear and tear!

Once the finished ball covers are dry, fill them
with millet or rice. This gives them the necessary
'weight' and means they drop into your hands
nicely while juggling.

After sewing the opening shut with tiny, near
invisible stitches, felt the seam again to make it
less obvious. If you want, you can decorate the
balls with glitter or sequins.

Note: If you want to make a set of identical balls,
weigh the wool and filling material beforehand, and
felt and full all the balls for the same length of time

24.1   *Juggling balls*

24.2   *Gnomes and 'Tiny swaddled dolls'*

Gnomes

(Shaped felt, felt ball)
- Cardboard template (see figure 24.3), allowing for shrinkage
- 5 g wool for the body (letter scales)
- 2 g wool for the head

Wind the wool in thin layers around the template, paying special attention to the tip of the hat.

After testing the felt, cut the package open at the bottom, remove the cardboard, turn the gnome inside out and felt the coloured outer side. Place the small body over two fingers, and felt it while rotating it around them. Massage the hat over the tip of your forefinger to make it nice and pointy. Make a small horizontal slit below the hat for inserting the head (see figure 24.3). To make the head see 'Felting small balls' page 34.

To finish, sew the head to the body with a few stitches. If the gnome does not stand well, cut the lower edges straight. Fill the coat with some wool. Run a string around the neck.

Note: By amending the template a little, you can use it to make finger puppets or standing dolls.

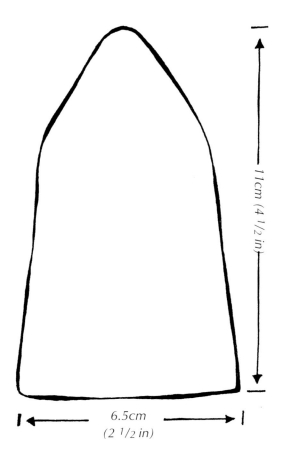

11cm (4 1/2 in)

6.5cm (2 1/2 in)

24.3   Gnome templates

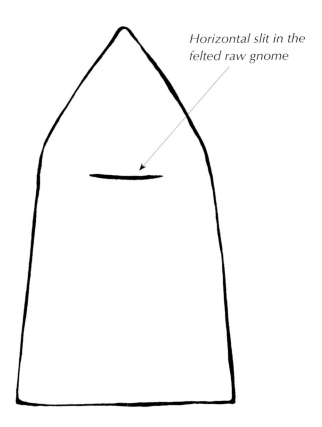

Horizontal slit in the felted raw gnome

Tiny swaddled dolls

(Shaped felt, felt ball)
- Small cardboard oval as a template (see figure 24.5)
- 2 g wool for the body (letter scales)
- 1.5 g wool for the head

Wind the wool around the small template and felt it between the palms of your hands. Try to avoid bulges at the edges even though the pieces are so small. Cut the slit for the head with a very sharp pair of scissors and remove the cardboard with tweezers. It is not possible to turn this tiny piece inside out. Stuff the body with some wool after it has dried.

Felt the head and attach it to the body as described for the gnomes (page 131). Use a length of wool yarn for the swaddling band.

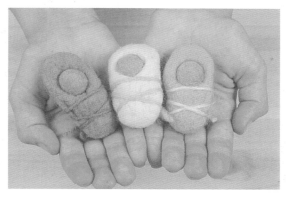

24.4   *Tiny swaddled dolls*

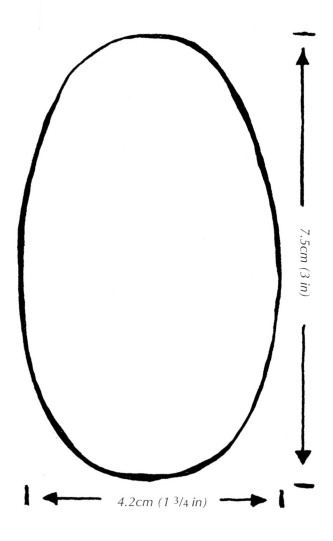

7.5cm (3 in)

4.2cm (1 ³/₄ in)

24.5   *Template measurements for 'Tiny swaddled dolls'*

Hand puppet

(Shaped felt, modelled felt, felt cords)

You can adapt this basic pattern to make any puppet you want. The measurements given are for a child's hand. A puppet to fit an adult hand will require a larger template and more wool.

- 70 g (2 ¹/₂ oz) wool for the entire puppet: mainly red and blue, some skin-coloured, some yellow wool for the hair
- Coloured felt shapes for decorating the garment and hat (cut them out of felt leftovers or a felt sheet)
- Wool for stuffing the head
- Blue and black embroidery thread
- Thick white and dark red wool yarn or felt cords to make the lips and eyes
- Cardboard for template (see figures 24.7 and 24.9)
- Needle with a very large eye
- 1 bell (optional)
- Red and light blue coloured pencils

Wet the coloured pieces of felt and spread them out over the template to make a nice pattern for the puppet's cloak. Wind red or blue wool in layers around the body and sleeves and felt. Wind skin coloured wool around the face and hands; overlap approximately 2 cm (³/₄ in) with the cloak to avoid gaps. Felt! Do not felt the head too much; it should remain soft so you can model the face later.

Make a slit along the hemline, remove the cardboard, turn it right side out and view your patterned puppet!

Felt the outside for several minutes (apart from the head). Rinse the puppet well and squeeze out excess water.

Stuff the still-wet head, poke a hole into the stuffing wool for your finger. Soap the face slightly. Gradually build up the nose, chin and cheeks using layers of skin-coloured wool. Model and massage until you are satisfied with it. Rinse out the soap well.

24.6   *Hand puppet*

133

Eyes

Outline the eyes with a thin black thread. Embroider a blue pupil, then sew the whites of the eyes to the left and right using thick yarn or felt cord. Do not sew beyond the borders of the black outline.

Mouth

Sew the upper and lower lip with dark red felt cord or yarn. Sew the corners of the mouth slightly upwards.

Hair

Make felt cords (see page 36) using different shades of yellow wool. Place them over the head and sew them on, one behind the other, along a central parting line until the hair is thick enough.

Hands

If you want, you can sew fingers using strong thread and a tight satin stitch.

Cap

Make the long pointed cap large enough. Arrange the felt shapes over the template (see figure 24.7) to make a pattern as described above for the cloak. Wind layers of coloured wool around the template and felt. Rinse the finished cap thoroughly.

Sew the cap to the head whilst still damp. Gather the hat at the back until it fits. If you want to be able to remove the hat, sew an elastic band around the base. Turn up the edge to make a small brim. Sew a bell to the tip (optional).

To finish, when the face is dry, shade in red cheeks. You can accentuate the eyelids with a light blue coloured pencil.

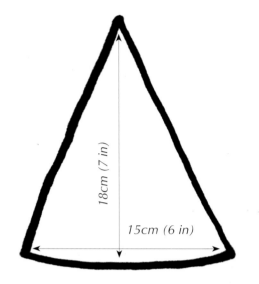

18cm (7 in)

15cm (6 in)

24.7   *Hand puppet's cap*

24.8   *Hand puppet*

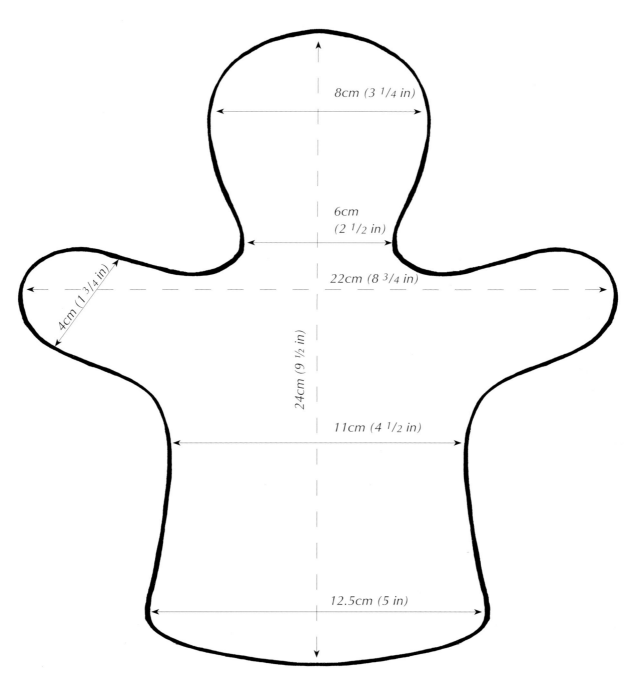

8cm (3 ¹/4 in)

6cm
(2 ¹/2 in)

22cm (8 3/4 in)

4cm (1 3/4 in)

24cm (9 ¹/2 in)

11cm (4 ¹/2 in)

12.5cm (5 in)

24.9   *Template for 'Hand puppet' (measurements for a child's hand)*

Finger puppets

(Shaped felt)

- Wool, any colour
- Skin-coloured wool
- Needle and thread
- Embroidery thread for the face
- Cardboard for the template

Cut the template out of cardboard: outline your finger and add about 1.5 cm (1/2 in) all the way round. Wind coloured wool firmly around the template to make the puppet's clothes. Wind skin-coloured wool around the top third for the head. Make sure there is no hole at the top. Overlap the skin-coloured wool with the garment to avoid any gaps. Start felting.

Cut open at the base, turn right side out and finish felting on your finger.

Add hair and if desired a hat. For instructions on how to make a hat, see 'Spring fairy' page 86. Sew eyes and mouth with a few stitches.

If the finger puppet is too long, trim the base or fold it up.

The tiny rabbit pictured in figure 24.10 is easy to make: take a strand of wool and tie two knots. Pull one end of the strand apart for the ears. Alternatively, felt a miniature egg and pull two bits of wool through the head to make ears.

24.10   *Finger puppets*

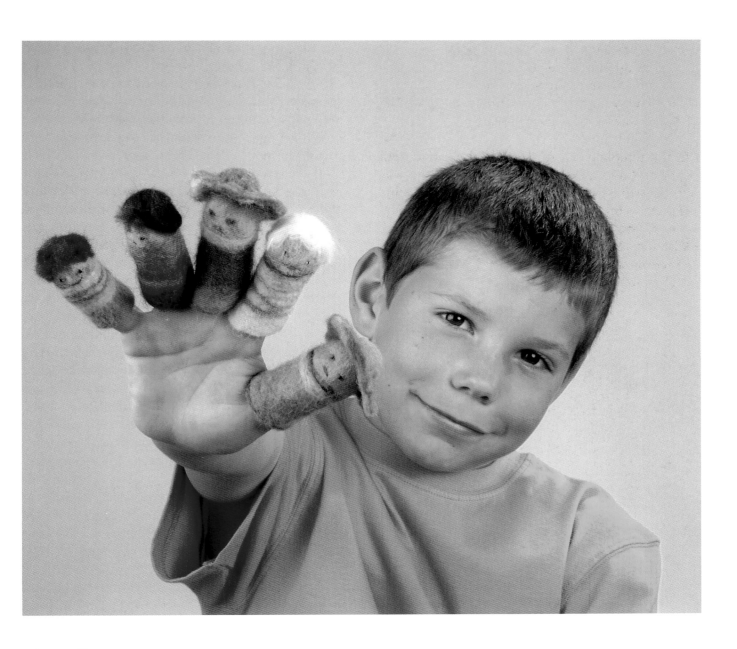

24.11   *Finger puppets*

24.12   *Heart bags*

Heart bags

(Shaped felt, flat felt)

These heart bags have been inspired by German gingerbread hearts, which are decorated with icing sugar and found at every German Christmas market. There is a slit in the back where you can put a gift or hide a treat (see page 108 for view of the back).

- Approximately 20 g (3/4 oz) red wool; white wool and any other colours for decoration
- Cardboard
- Ribbon for suspending
- Needle with a large eye

Cut the heart-shaped template out of cardboard (see figure 24.20).

Felt small flat pieces of coloured felt between your palms; do not make them too thin. Cut shapes or letters out of these pieces of felt.

Place wet, thin strands of white wool as a decorative border around the edge of the template. Wavy lines are particularly attractive and not difficult to make. Wet the felt shapes or letters and lay them on the template in the desired pattern. See figures 24.13–24.19 for step-by-step instructions on how to felt a pattern to shaped felt.

Note: remember to mirror write words when laying down letters!

Once the decorations are all in place, lay the first thin, red wool layer over the top, wet, press down with soapy hands and felt for a few minutes. This should connect the pattern to the red wool sufficiently so that it doesn't slip.

Turn the template over. Smooth the overhanging wool over the edges. Layer more red wool over the side without the pattern until all the wool has been evenly distributed around the heart.

Note: Once the heart is entirely wrapped in red wool, you will not be able to see which is the patterned side. To prevent cutting open the wrong (patterned) side, always mark the reverse side by placing a different coloured bit of wool on each layer.

Felt gently initially, then more vigorously. Pay particular attention to the tip and groove of the heart to make sure there are no holes or bulges anywhere.

The felt is finished once it has passed the *felting test* (see page 30).

Cut a horizontal slit approximately 7 cm (2 3/4 in) into the top third of the back of the finished heart. Remove the cardboard, turn the heart right side out. Place one hand inside and shape well. If there is a hole at the tip or if the edges appear transparent, add some red wool from the inside and felt on as well as possible. Re-felt the patterned side and the cut edges.

To finish, attach a ribbon to the bag using a needle with a large eye.

How to felt a pattern to shaped felt

24.13 1. Place the pattern (letters in mirror writing) onto the template

24.14 2. Place the first layer of wool over it, press down, rub gently

24.15 3. Turn the template over, smooth the overhanging wool over the edges

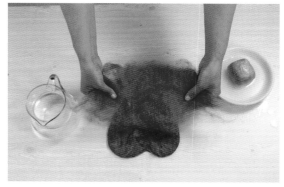

24.16 4. Place a layer of wool over the back and mark with a small different coloured bit of wool.

24.17 5. Once it has felted sufficiently (felt test) cut a small slit into the back

24.18 6. Remove the cardboard, turn the heart right side out

24.19 7. Re-felt the front side and if necessary make small corrections

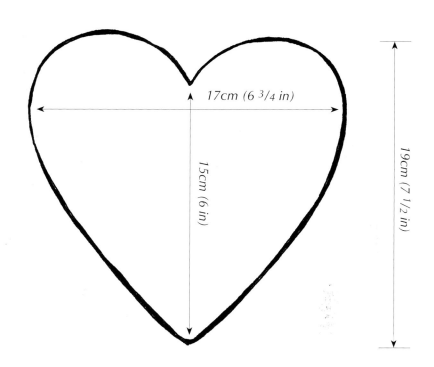

17cm (6 3/4 in)

15cm (6 in)

19cm (7 1/2 in)

24.20 Heart bag

Teddy bear

(Shaped felt, flat felt)

This teddy bear has been designed to look like a vintage bear from over a hundred years ago. Plastic joints give it a movable head, arms and legs. Teddy bears are a lot of fun to make and each one is unique. The bears pictured were both made following the same pattern, and yet have completely different looks. Hand felted bears are durable and hard-wearing They are not suitable for very young children due to small parts like eyes and joints. Older children and adult bear collectors will enjoy them greatly.

For a bear approximately 27 cm (10 ½ in) tall. Head with ears approximately 20 g; body approximately 30 g; both front legs together approximately 15 g; both hind legs together approximately 25 g.

- Approximately 90 g (3 ¼ oz) fur-coloured wool
- Approximately 100 g (3 ½ oz) white wool for stuffing
- Orange or beige wool to felt the paws and ears
- Embroidery thread (dark brown, black or dark blue)
- Thin, stiff cardboard

24.21   *Teddy bears' picnic*

- 1 set of plastic joints
- 1 pair of glass eyes with metal loop at the back (small black or dark blue button eyes without pupils are best for this bear)
- Strong thread and 1 long needle with a large eye

(Purchase the last four items from a craft shop)

Plastic joints

For a bear this size, you will need plastic joints as follows:

- Head 40 mm
- Front legs 30 mm
- Hind legs 35 mm

If you cannot obtain these exact sizes, use slightly smaller discs. Plastic joints are usually sold in sets. Once the joints are fitted together, they cannot be separated again. Make sure that when you push them together they are positioned correctly. It is helpful to take the finished felted arms and legs to your craft store and ask for advice.

Note: Take the wool allocated for front and hind legs and divide each amount into two equal portions so that both front legs and both hind legs are felted with the same quantity of wool and are the same size and thickness.

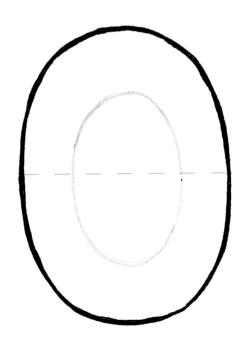

24.22   *Ear template x 1 for both ears*

24.23   *Inner ear template x 1 for both ears*

How to make the teddy bear

Cut out the cardboard templates (see figures 24.22–24.27).

Lightly felt a flat sheet out of orange or beige wool about 4 mm thick. Cut out paws, soles and inner ears (see figures 24.23 and 24.25). Wet all these pieces well. Place the ears and paws onto the correct places on the template (see figures 24.22 and 24.24). They will remain in place quite reliably (see photo page 147).

Fold the wet soles in half lengthwise and place them over the edge of the base of the foot template.

Note: Both ears are made using a single template which is then cut in half once felted.

Spread the fur-coloured wool evenly and without gaps over the templates, making sure the orange parts below do not slip out of place. Always lay thin layers of wool. Wet each layer with warm water, press down with soapy hands and shape firmly around the template. Felt each part for the same length of time and intensity, until the felt is firm and stable, apart from the head.

Do not felt the head as long and energetically as the rest. It needs to remain slightly soft so you can finish felting it with the help of a round object.

Cut slits into the different body parts to remove the cardboard and for stuffing later:
- On the back approximately 7 cm (2 3/4 in)
- Back of front legs approximately 4 cm (1 1/2 in)
- Back of hind legs approximately 5 cm (2 in)

- Cut the neck slit straight across the lower edge of the template
- Cut the ear template in half

Turn all parts right side out. Check whether the orange paws and ears have felted on well and re-felt.

Shape the head over a round or oval object, for example a small ball, large darning egg, or similar household object. The light grey bear's head, for example, was shaped over a lemon. It is sometimes necessary to carefully add more thin layers of wool to the head, particularly the back of the head and cheeks. Remember the new wool can only connect well to the base if the head has not been felted too much already! To shape the head, push the round or oval object through the neck hole into the pre-felted head, soap and gently massage. Stroke and model the nose into shape. The neck opening will often contract while felting, and it is necessary to cut a new slit to remove the object inside. Sew this slit shut before stuffing the head. Rinse the finished head well and let it dry.

Divide the 100 g of stuffing wool into six approximately equal parts. First, stuff the head with one part, making sure the snout is firmly stuffed too. Using strong thread, run a gathering thread around the edge of the neck. Insert the largest joint washer into the opening, with the stem pointing outside the head. Push the washer up against the stuffing wool. Tighten the gathering thread until the washer has completely disappeared and the neck opening is fully shut. Sew in the end of the thread securely and put the head to one side.

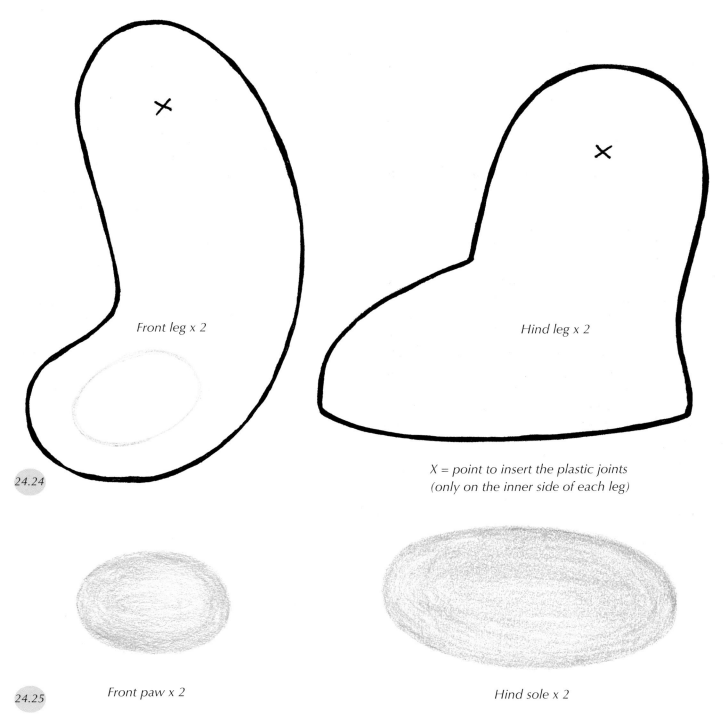

Front leg x 2

Hind leg x 2

X = point to insert the plastic joints
(only on the inner side of each leg)

24.24

24.25

Front paw x 2

Hind sole x 2

145

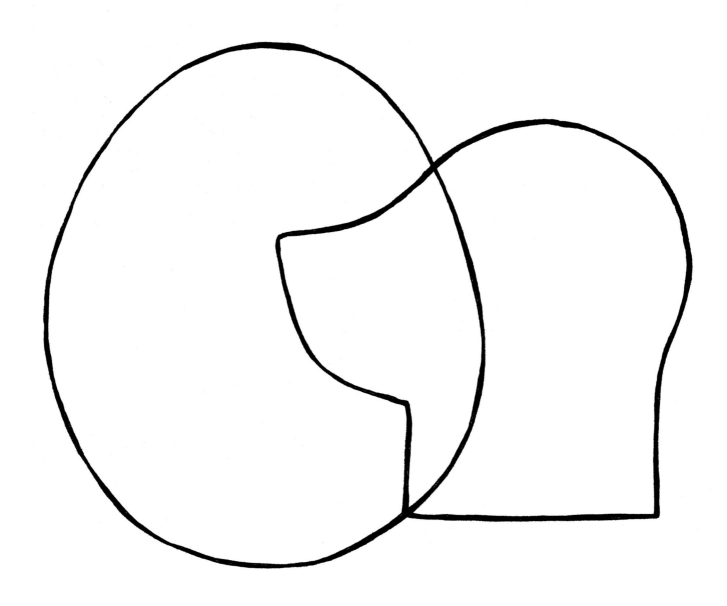

24.26   *Body x 1*   24.27   *Head x 1*

Make a hole, large enough to fit the joint stems, at the top inside of the front legs and hind legs with a sharp object. See figure 24.24 for the exact position of the holes. Place the disks with the stems in the front and hind legs *before stuffing*, pushing the stems through the holes.

Note: Do not inadvertently make two left front or hind legs. The orange coloured paws and the stems sticking out the front legs should both be facing the body.

Stuff front and hind legs, remembering to stuff the tips of feet and paws well. Stuff firmly around the joints too. Using a strong thread, sew the seams shut with small stitches.

Determine where to join the front and hind legs to the body before stuffing the body. Make holes in the body at these points using a sharp object. Push the stems of front and hind legs into these holes; the stems now stick into the body. Re-check whether the front and hind legs are positioned at the same height and in the correct places. Move the limbs, examine the half-finished bear from all sides and sit it down. If you are not satisfied, make new holes. Once assembled, the joints cannot be corrected any more!

When you are happy with how the bear looks, attach the other side of the joints to the stems from the inside of the body, until arm and leg joints are tightly connected but move smoothly.

1. Ear template, later cut in half to make two ears
2. Weighed amount of wool for the head
3. Weighed amount of wool for the front legs
4. Weighed amount of wool for the body
5. Weighed amount of wool for both hind legs
6. Wet the sole ovals and fold them around the template

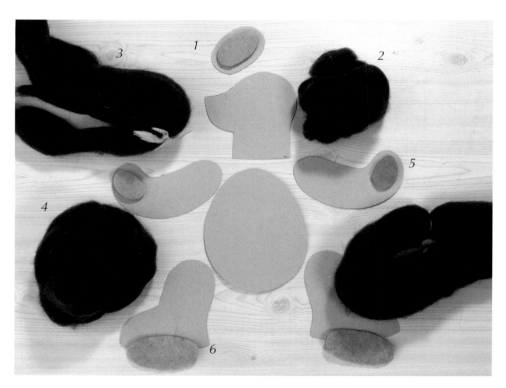

24.28   *All the templates with corresponding felt*

147

Determine the correct point between the shoulders for attaching the head to the body. Make a hole and push the head stem through it. Push the other side of the joint to the stem from within the body as described above for the legs. Stuff the body with the remaining wool and the seam at the back. You can re-felt all the seams to make them less noticeable.

Do not place the ears too far forward into the forehead or too close together. Shape the base of the ears into a slight curve and sew them to the head, sewing right around the base of the ear with small, tight stitches.

Embroider the nose with horizontal, closely placed satin stitches.

To make a friendly smile, first sew a vertical stitch below the finished nose, then sew two further stitches to the right and left of it, angled slightly upwards.

Determine the position of the eyes by sticking two glass-headed pins into the head. The best place is usually along the line where the bridge of the nose meets the forehead. Do not place the eyes too high up on the forehead. Once you are satisfied with the position, make a hole in the felt with a large knitting needle. Thread strong thread into the extra long needle and push it up from the neck, beside the joint, leaving a few centimetres of thread hanging loose at the neck. Push the needle through the head and emerge at the hole that you made with the knitting needle. Thread the needle through the eye loop, push the needle back into the hole and down through the head to the neck again.

Pull both thread ends together tightly at the neck. Pull until the loop disappears completely into the head, and the eyes are fastened securely and lie firmly in the eye sockets. Secure the thread with several knots and sew in the thread ends. Use a second thread for the second eye and attach in the same way as described above.

To finish, sew eyebrows and claws with satin stitch.

24.29 *Bear ready to assemble with joint and eyes*

Fried eggs

(For doll's kitchen and teddy bears' picnic)
Felt a small amount of white wool between the palms of your hands (egg white). Felt a small soft yellow ball for the egg yolk. Sew the yolk to the centre of the egg white with a few stitches to stop it slipping. Continue felting between the palms of your hands for a few minutes. If necessary, trim the egg white, then briefly re-felt the edges. Finished!

24.30   *Fried eggs*

Fish music box

(Shaped felt, flat felt)
- Approximately 30 g (1 oz) blue or dark violet wool
- Some coloured strands of wool for the face and tail
- Approximately 10 g ($^1/_3$ oz) coloured wool to make bits of flat felt (or scraps of leftover felt) for the scales; choose colours that contrast with blue or violet.
- Approximately 40 g (1 $^1/_2$ oz) wool for stuffing
- Cardboard
- Needle and thread
- Music box with pull string (craft or toy shop)

It is best to buy the music box first, so you can make the fish to fit it. Cut the fish template out of cardboard (see figure 24.32). Cut the scales out of coloured pieces of felt.

Tail
Wet long staple wool strands and press them to the cardboard to make a striped pattern. Wind a wet strand of wool around the base of the tail to contrast with the body.

Face
Wet two red tufts of wool, not too thin, and place on the template for the lips. Wrap a wet strand of wool around your finger to make a ring for the eye. Place a differently coloured bit of wool inside the eye. Wind a wet strand around the head to contrast with the body in the same way as the tail.

Carefully lay the scales over one side of the template. Spread a layer of blue or violet wool out over the whole fish. Wet and gently felt on with soapy hands. Once the scales have lightly felted to the top layer of wool, turn the template over. Lay the scales over the other side of the template in the same way, then smooth the overhanging wet wool from the first side around the edges of the template. Place another layer of wool over the scales, wet, soap and felt. Add several more layers. Felt the evenly covered fish and keep smoothing around the edges so the scales do not slip.

Cut a slit into the bottom of the stomach, just large enough for the music box to fit through, and turn the fish right side out. Re-felt the outer side. Push one hand into the fish and shape the lips and tail.

For further instructions, see 'Star music box' page 110.

24.31   *Fish music box*

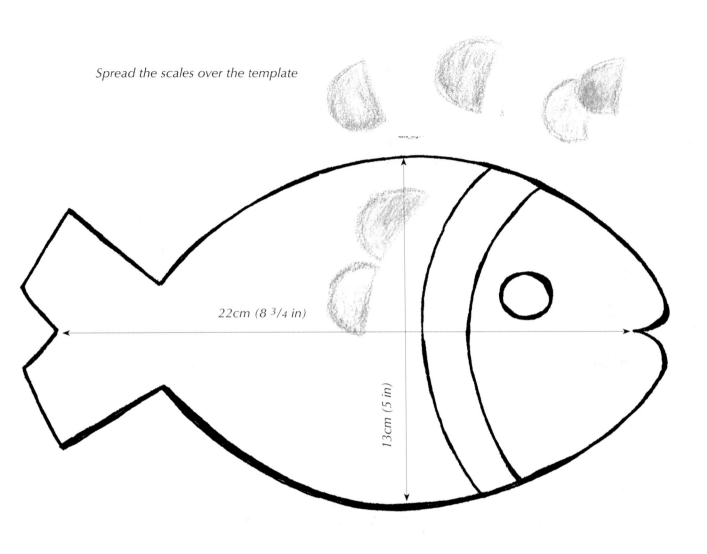

Spread the scales over the template

22cm (8 3/4 in)

13cm (5 in)

24.32 *Cardboard template for 'Fish music box'*

Fleece shawl

The basis of this lovely shawl was a beautiful, freshly shorn moorland sheep fleece. Overall, it was carefully washed twice. In the centre was a connecting piece that coincidentally looked like a shawl. This part was carefully teased away from the rest once the fleece had dried. The skin side had a lot of 'felt friendly' underwool. The whole shawl was still reinforced with a layer of milk sheep wool. Thinner areas received an extra layer of wool, and then the felting process began. The long, smooth wool on the outside did not felt, but was still sufficiently connected to the under wool.

It is a lot easier for two people to work on such a large area. Towards the end, you can use your feet to help!

When making such a large felt item, sometimes areas do not felt together well and start to pull apart. If this happens, sew the gaps together with a needle and thread.

- Weight of the shawl about 500 g (1 lb)
- Felting time: about one to two afternoons outside

24.33   Fleece shawl

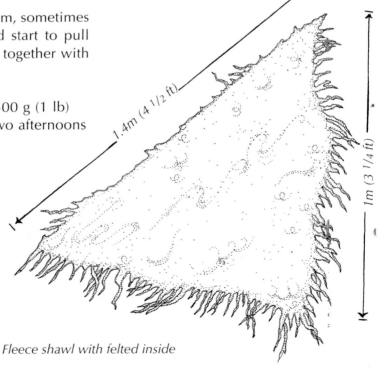

1.4m (4 1/2 ft)

1m (3 1/4 ft)

24.34   Fleece shawl with felted inside